13 Society for people wh
high in intelligence tests.   M . . . .

Ken Russell is a London surveyor who lives in Kent. He
is the Puzzle Editor of *Mensa*, a magazine issued free
each month to Mensa's 20,000 UK members.

Philip Carter is a Yorkshire estimator and a Justice of
the Peace. He is Puzzle Editor of *Enigmasig*, the
magazine for the Mensa Puzzle Special Interest Group.

Also in Sphere Books by Philip Carter and Ken Russell:

THE MENSA PUZZLE BOOK
THE MENSA PUZZLE BOOK 2
THE JUNIOR MENSA PUZZLE BOOK
THE IQ TEST BOOK

The Mensa General Knowledge Quiz Book

Philip Carter
Ken Russell

SPHERE BOOKS LIMITED

A Sphere Book

First published in Great Britain by Sphere Books Ltd 1989
1st reprint 1990

Printed and bound in Great Britain by
BPCC Hazell Books
Aylesbury, Bucks, England
Member of BPCC Ltd.

ISBN 0 7474 0181 0

Sphere Books Ltd
A Division of
Macdonald & Co (Publishers) Ltd
Orbit House
1 New Fetter Lane
London EC4A 1AR
A member of Maxwell Macmillan Pergamon Publishing Corporation

Author's Note

This book is dedicated to our wives, both named Barbara, who have given us their support and encouragement in our endeavour to compile new and interesting puzzles, and have checked out the answers.

We also wish to acknowledge the assistance and advice given to us by Victor Serebriakoff, the International President of Mensa, who is a great puzzle innovator. We are indebted too to Harold Gale, the Mensa Chief Executive, a prolific puzzle composer, and we wish to thank the members of the British Mensa Committee who gave permission for use of the Mensa name in the title.

What Is Mensa?

Mensa is a unique society. It is, basically, a social club – but a social club different from others. The only qualification for membership is a high score on an intelligence test. One person in fifty should qualify for membership; these people will come from all walks of life and have a wide variety of interests and occupations.

Mensa is the Latin word for table: we are a round-table society where no one has special precedence. We fill a void for many intelligent people otherwise cut off from contact with other good minds – contact that is important to them, but elusive in modern society. Besides being an origin of many new friendships, we provide members with a receptive but critical audience on which to try out new ideas.

Mensa is protean: its most visible feature is its diversity. It crosses the often artificial barriers which separate people from each other. It recruits, not like other societies by persuading people to think as they do, or by searching for a particularly narrow common interest, but by scientifically selecting people who are able to think for themselves. Yet, although there appears little common ground and little surface agreement between members, we find there is an underlying unity which gives an unexpected strength to the society.

Mensa has three aims: social contact between intelligent people; research in psychology and the social sciences; and the identification and fostering of human intelligence. Mensa is an international society; it has more than 85,000 members. We have members of almost every occupation – business people, clerks, doctors, editors, factory workers, farm labourers, housewives, lawyers, police officers, politicians, soldiers, scientists, students, teachers – and of almost every age.

Enquiries and applications to:

Mensa
FREEPOST
Wolverhampton WV2 1BR

Mensa International
15 The Ivories
6–8 Northampton Street
London N1 2HV

Each answer begins with the letter on the right: each dot stands for a letter. Scoring for each quiz is included in the answers section.

Scoring for quiz one as follows:

10–12	Fair
13–17	Good
18–21	Very good
22–24	Excellent

Each subsequent quiz progressively increases in difficulty and scoring is gradually adjusted accordingly.

1 Study of stars in relation to human affairs.

A . . . .

2 Unit of dry measure containing four pecks.

B . . . . .

3 Wife of an earl.

C . . . .

4 Australian wolf-like dog.

D . . . .

5 Northern stoat whose fur turns white in winter.

E . . . . . .

6 Conversion of liquid into solid form.

F . . . .

7 Explosive invented in 9th-century China.

G . . . .

8 What travels by conduction, convection and radiation?

H . . .

9 What in America connects a war, a declaration and a town in Missouri?

I . . . .

10 Son of Mary Queen of Scots.

J . . . .

11 What in Moscow is 'the city within a city'?

K . . . . . .

12 Divisional unit of a Roman army.

L . . . . .

13 Dickens character who hoped something would turn up.

M . . . .

14 Sentimental longing for times gone by.

N . . . .

15 A cuttle-fish with eight arms.

O . . . . . .

16 What is associated with Shrove Tuesday?

P . . . .

17 Game in which a ring is thrown over a peg.

Q . . . . .

18   Who was known as 'coeur de lion'?   R . . . .

19   American inventor who patented sewing machine in 1851.   S . . . . .

20   Light war-hatchet.   T . . . .

21   Imaginary island of Sir Thomas More's romance (1516).   U . . . . .

22   Who married Albert of Saxe-Coburg-Gotha in 1840?   V . . . .

23   Lord Mayor of London in 1397, 1406 and 1419.   W . . . .

24   Form of singing which changes from ordinary voice to falsetto.   Y . . . .

TWO

No.	Clue	Answer
1	Food of the gods.	A . . . .
2	Two footed animal.	B . . . .
3	Grounds of university.	C . . . . .
4	Piece of turf.	D . . . .
5	Head of corn.	E . .
6	Bundle of sticks.	F . . . . .
7	Drink or eat greedily.	G . . . . .
8	Type of melon.	H . . . .
9	Eskimo's domed hut.	I . . . .
10	Large thick skinned orange.	J . . . .
11	Twist in wire or chain.	K . . .
12	Matter flowing from volcano.	L . . .
13	Large residence.	M . . . . . .
14	Synthetic textile fabric.	N . . . .

15	Wet mud or slime.	O . . .
16	Light umbrella.	P . . . . .
17	Ignorant pretender in medicine.	Q . . . .
18	Rare, red, precious stone.	R . . .
19	Move stealthily.	S . . . .
20	Group of oxen.	T . . .
21	Open sore.	U . . . .
22	Calf's flesh.	V . . .
23	Adore.	W . . . . . .
24	Light sailing vessel.	Y . . . .

THREE

1	On what horse did Bob Champion achieve his famous 1981 Grand National victory?	A . . . .
2	Secret method of voting.	B . . . . .
3	Illustration of a satirical or humorous character.	C . . . . . .
4	Unit for measuring loudness of sound.	D . . . . . .
5	What plant's name means 'noble white'?	E . . . .
6	English ballerina who was originally Margaret Hookham.	F . . . . . .
7	A young goose.	G . . . . . .
8	Gas which combined with oxygen produces water.	H . . . .
9	One who assumes a false character.	I . . . .
10	City captured by Joshua and the Israelites.	J . . . . .

11 Sacred book of Islam.   K . . . .

12 A rope with a noose at one
end.   L . . . . .

13 What metal was named after
a Roman god?   M . . . . . .

14 Patron saint of children.   N . . . .

15 Which French city was saved
by Joan of Arc?   O . . . . . .

16 The collection and study of
postage stamps.   P . . . .

17 A composition for four voices
or instruments.   Q . . . . . .

18 Who set out to write a world
history whilst a prisoner in the
Tower of London?   R . . . . . .

19 What word connects
contract, class and security?   S . . . . .

20 Nickname of *The Times*
newspaper.   T . . . .

21 Latin name for Odysseus.   U . . . . . .

22 Textile fabric with long silk
nap.   V . . . . .

23 What distinctive name is
given to the house at 1600
Pennsylvania Avenue?   W . . . .

24 A country bumpkin.   Y . . . .

FOUR

1 In Greek legend a race of
warrior women.   A . . . . . .

2 Large African monkey.   B . . . . .

3 Cotton cloth.   C . . . . .

4

4	Large extinct bird of Mauritius.	D . . .
5	Female sheep.	E . .
6	One side of a many-sided body.	F . . . .
7	Zest, enjoyment.	G . . . .
8	Reaping machine.	H . . . .
9	Child of the devil.	I . .
10	Fast lively jazz dance.	J . . .
11	Small barrel.	K . .
12	Which animal is 'king of the beasts'?	L . . .
13	What is the capital of Spain?	M . . . . .
14	12 o'clock of the day.	N . . .
15	Sphere or globe.	O . .
16	Minister in charge of church.	P . . . . .
17	Drink deeply.	Q . . . .
18	Thin slice of bacon or ham.	R . . . . .
19	Afternoon nap or rest in Spain.	S . . . . .
20	Elephant's tooth.	T . . .
21	Vase with feet.	U . .
22	Rascal.	V . . . . .
23	Flat purse.	W . . . . .
24	White metallic element.	Z . . .

FIVE

| 1 | Substances which turn litmus blue. | A . . . . . . |
| 2 | Vessel in which water is strongly heated. | B . . . . |

3 Council composed of principal members of the British Government.

C . . . .

4 Transparent crystal of pure carbon.

D . . . . . .

5 Conversion of liquid into vapour.

E . . . .

6 How many British kings have there been this century?

F . . .

7 A Japanese dancing-girl.

G . . . . .

8 The art of cultivating gardens.

H . . . .

9 A triangle in which two sides are equal.

I . . . .

10 A rally of scouts.

J . . . .

11 What word connects up, down and out?

K . . . .

12 What famous statue is found on Bedloe's Island?

L . . . . . .

13 Independent principality on the Riviera coast.

M . . . . .

14 The centre of an atom.

N . . . . . .

15 Pseudonym of Eric Arthur Blair (1903–50).

O . . . . .

16 A five-pointed star.

P . . . .

17 The minimum number of persons required to render a meeting valid.

Q . . . . .

18 Vulgar sign of disapproval formed by blowing with the tongue between the lips.

R . . . .

19 Son of Mary Arden.

S . . . .

20 Whose tomb was discovered near Luxor in 1922?

T . . . .

21 Last month.   U . . . . .

22 The amount of space
occupied by any material.   V . . . . .

23 The seat of the Lord
Chancellor in the House of Lords.   W . . . .

24 International phonetic code
name for 'X'.   X . . .

SIX
_____

1 What is the only American
state with 'z' in its name?   A . . . . . .

2 Original name for a
madhouse.   B . . . . .

3 Highland sport – tossing the
- - - - -.   C . . . .

4 Farm horse.   D . . . . .

5 Set in order for publication.   E . . .

6 Musical term signifying 'loud'.   F . . . .

7 Large rich cream cake.   G . . . . .

8 Old English single-step sailor's
dance.   H . . . .

9 Image or statue.   I . . .

10 Practical joke.   J . . .

11 Bone at finger joint.   K . . . . . .

12 Machine for shaping wood or
metal.   L . . . .

13 Medieval musician.   M . . . .

14 Name for a donkey.   N . . . .

15 Man-eating giant.   O . . .

16 Of the Pope.   P . . . .

17 Strongest piece in chess.   Q . . . .

18	Fabulous bird.	R . .
19	Staying power.	S . . . . . .
20	Bull fighter.	T . . . .
21	Overturn.	U . . . .
22	Country residence.	V . . . .
23	Fermented grape juice.	W . . .
24	Japanese monetary unit.	Y . .

SEVEN

1 What was the name of the first yacht to win the America's cup?   A . . . . . .

2 Only mammal to have power of active flight.   B . .

3 Science which examines the composition and qualities of all kinds of matter.   C . . . .

4 Electric current which always flows in the same direction.   D . . . . .

5 A cake long in shape with cream filling and chocolate covering.   E . . . . .

6 Who was created by Mary Shelley?   F . . . .

7 What word connects an English coin and a small rodent?   G . . . . .

8 Eve of All Saint's Day.   H . . . .

9 Deceptive appearance.   I . . . .

10 American brothers who robbed banks and trains during 1870s.   J . . . .

11 Unit of speed used by ships.   K . . .

12 Tenancy of property limited to a certain number of years. L . . . .

13 Second order in the English peerage. M . . . . . .

14 Capital of Bahamas. N . . . . .

15 Which mollusc produces the most eggs per year? O . . . . .

16 Italian composer of *La Bohème*. P . . . . . .

17 Any four-footed animal. Q . . . .

18 Russian holy man assassinated in Petrograd. R . . . .

19 Nickname of Thomas Jonathan Jackson, American Civil War general. S . . . .

20 Card game used mainly for fortune-telling. T . . . .

21 Small four-stringed guitar of Portuguese origin. U . . . . . .

22 Group of organic compounds essential to normal body metabolism. V . . . .

23 What is catch-as-catch-can? W . . . .

24 Sea which is an arm of the Pacific between China and Korea. Y . . . . .

EIGHT

1 What is the largest American river? A . . . . .

2 Belltower. B . . . . .

3 Hiding place for treasure. C . . . .

4 Small boat. D . . . . .

5 Run away to get married.	E . . . .
6 Cruel, wicked, person.	F . . . .
7 Raise price of house after accepting offer.	G . . . . .
8 Oriental smoking pipe.	H . . . . .
9 Entrails.	I . . . . . .
10 Sportsman's light spear.	J . . . . . .
11 Large bird of prey.	K . . .
12 Breed of retriever dog.	L . . . .
13 Emperor of Japan.	M . . . . .
14 Recess.	N . . .
15 Fertile spot in desert.	O . . . .
16 Straw bed or mattress.	P . . . . .
17 Search for object or idea.	Q . . . .
18 Hindu Queen.	R . . . .
19 Fairy.	S . . . . .
20 South American dance.	T . . . .
21 Indefinitely many.	U . . . . . .
22 Short curtain.	V . . . . . .
23 Nutritious cereal.	W . . . .
24 Mammal living at high altitude.	Y . .

NINE

1 Capital of Jordan.	A . . . .
2 Ship sent to Tahiti in 1787 under command of Lieut. William Bligh.	B . . . . .
3 The numbering of a country's population on the same day.	C . .

4   Kind of thick pudding or mass of soft paste.

D . . . .

5   Study of production, distribution and consumption of commodities.

E . . . .

6   Birthplace of Florence Nightingale.

F . . . .

7   Science which deals with the composition and structure of the earth's crust.

G . . . . . .

8   A young cow.

H . . . . .

9   Near at hand.

I . . . .

10   Which Virginian wrote the Declaration of Independence?

J . . . .

11   Soviet political leader during 1962 Cuban missile crisis.

K . . . .

12   Textile fabric woven out of flax threads.

L . . . . .

13   What word connects a fruit and a Chinese official?

M . . . .

14   Long fictional prose narrative.

N . . . . .

15   Orchestral prelude.

O . . . .

16   Who wrote *Tales of Mystery and Imagination*?

P . .

17   Period of isolation to prevent infection.

Q . . . .

18   Wind instrument of flute type.

R . . . .

19   On which motor racing circuit would you find Becketts, Abbey and Club?

S . . . .

20   Pen name of American writer Samuel Langhorne Clemens.

T . . . . .

21 Mammary gland of cow, goat and other mammals. U . . . .

22 Only poisonous snake indigenous to Britain. V . . . .

23 Who originated the term 'horse-power'? W . . .

24 Mormon leader who promulgated the doctrine of polygamy. Y . . . .

TEN

1 Small counting frame. A . . . . .

2 What is the capital of Switzerland? B . . . .

3 Card game. C . . . . . .

4 False shirt front. D . . . .

5 Small whirlpool. E . . .

6 Plate over shop front with owner's name. F . . . .

7 Hindu spiritual teacher. G . . .

8 Canopied seat on an elephant. H . . . . .

9 Meanwhile. I . . . . . .

10 Caretaker of building. J . . . . . .

11 Dog's shelter. K . . . . .

12 West Indian dance. L . . . .

13 Infantry soldier's light gun. M . . . . .

14 Woman's loose informal garment. N . . . .

15 Burden. O . . .

16 One who defends his country. P . . . . . .

17 Game bird related to the partridge.   Q . . . .

18 Small stream.   R . . . . . .

19 Open weave cotton fabric.   S . . . .

20 System of weights for precious stones.   T . . .

21 Officer of court to conduct people.   U . . . .

22 Ballroom dance in triple time.   V . . . . .

23 Magician.   W . . . . .

24 Sweet potato.   Y . .

ELEVEN

1 What type of plants are Godetia, Lobelia, Nemesia and Petunia?   A . . . . . .

2 Who was Edward Teach better known as?   B . . . .

3 Which country's old name was Cathay?   C . . . .

4 Form of language peculiar to a district.   D . . . . . .

5 Competitive sport for horse and rider.   E . . . .

6 Originator of psycho-analysis.   F . . . .

7 Natural fountain of hot water.   G . . . . .

8 A large kind of wasp.   H . . . . .

9 The manager of a theatrical company.   I . . . .

10 English form of Yahweh, the Jewish name for God.   J . . . . . .

11 Small cubes of meat served on skewers.

K . . . .

12 The scientific study of reasoning.

L . . . .

13 What type of museum is at Greenwich Park in London?

M . . . .

14 Welsh composer and playwright whose works include *The Dancing Years*.

N . . . . . .

15 Type of pancake made chiefly with eggs.

O . . . .

16 The making of a false statement on oath.

P . . . . . .

17 The rules of boxing.

Q . . . .

18 Ninth month of Moslem year.

R . . . . . .

19 Who wrote *Man and Superman*?

S . . .

20 What comedian made his variety debut in 1922, at Collin's music hall, billed as Red Nirt?

T . . . . . .

21 What name connects a bird, a tree and a grass?

U . . . .

22 A common, as distinguished from a decimal, fraction.

V . . . . .

23 Small racing dog.

W . . . . . .

24 Royal bodyguard of England instituted (1485) by Henry VII.

Y . . . . .

TWELVE

1 First Greek letter of the alphabet.

A . . . .

14

2	Female ballet dancer.	B . . . .
3	Glass bottle.	C . . . . .
4	Long dagger.	D . . .
5	The best.	E . . . .
6	Pancake, sweet oatcake.	F . . . .
7	Birthstone for January.	G . . . . .
8	Large flat fish.	H . . . . . .
9	Wild goat with large curved horns.	I . . .
10	Sleeveless jacket.	J . . . . .
11	Open-fronted structure.	K . . . .
12	Weariness.	L . . . .
13	Optical illusion caused by atmospheric conditions.	M . . . . .
14	Strips of dough made of flour and eggs.	N . . . . . .
15	Cash.	O . .
16	Model of excellence.	P . . . . . .
17	Take exception and argue.	Q . . . . . .
18	Meeting for boats and yachts.	R . . . . . .
19	Lively jazz dance with heavy stamping.	S . . . .
20	Brass wind instrument.	T . . .
21	Person chosen to enforce rules.	U . . . . .
22	Humble dependent slave.	V . . . . .
23	Entirely.	W . . . . .
24	Comically idiotic.	Z . . .

THIRTEEN

1   Where would you find Hot Springs and Little Rock?

A . . . .

2   What synthetic resin was discovered in 1909 by Dr Leo Henrick Baekeland?

B . . . .

3   Who discovered the island of Cuba?

C . . . .

4   Trees which shed their leaves in autumn.

D . . . .

5   A state of even balance.

E . . . .

6   Which entertainer was born William Claude Dukinfield in Philadelphia (1880)?

F . . . . .

7   What river is sacred to Hindus?

G . . . . .

8   British composer whose works include the orchestral suite *The Planets*.

H . . . .

9   Hereditary rulers of Peru preceding the Spanish conquest in 1532.

I . . . .

10   International phonetic code name for 'j'.

J . . . . .

11   Scene of violent volcanic eruption in 1883.

K . . . .

12   British romantic writer of *Sons and Lovers*.

L . . . .

13   Stringed instrument.

M . . . .

14   Light and quick in motion.

N . . . . .

15   Sport combining navigation and cross-country running.

O . . . .

16

16   Which famous London theatre in Argyll Street was built as a variety house in 1910?   P . . . .

17   A state of perplexity.   Q . . . .

18   Language of gypsies.   R . . . . .

19   Which famous American composer of marches wrote *Liberty Bell?*   S . . . .

20   A large dish for holding food at the table.   T . . . . .

21   A mischievous child.   U . . . . .

22   An enclosed space containing no matter.   V . . . . .

23   What name connects a bird with St Paul's Cathedral?   W . . .

24   Animal resembling man, said to live in the Himalayas.   Y . . .

FOURTEEN

1   White of an egg.   A . . . . . .

2   Smear with paint.   B . . . . .

3   Secret intrigue.   C . . . .

4   Huge extinct reptile.   D . . . . . .

5   Small piece of live coal or wood.   E . . . .

6   Small fleet of boats.   F . . . .

7   Light flat-bottomed boat in Venice.   G . . . . . .

8   Dealer in small articles of dress.   H . . . .

9   Large lizard found in South America.   I . . . . .

10 Very short time.   J . . . .

11 One of noble birth raised in rank by king.   K . . . . .

12 Towards the sheltered side.   L . . . . . .

13 Fine delicately woven cotton fabric.   M . . . . .

14 Roaming from place to place.   N . . . .

15 Sex appeal.   O . . . .

16 Indian baby.   P . . . . . .

17 One of four children at birth.   Q . . . .

18 Round up of cattle on a ranch.   R . . . .

19 Cease to employ, set aside.   S . . . .

20 Table with three legs.   T . . . . .

21 Sense of slight or injury.   U . . . . . .

22 Female fox.   V . . . .

23 Joint connecting hand with forearm.   W . . . .

24 Plant with sword-like leaves.   Y . . . .

FIFTEEN

1 Artificial channel for conducting water from one place to another.   A . . . .

2 What creature do you connect with Col. W. F. Cody?   B . . . . . .

3 From what plant is hashish and marijuana obtained?   C . . . .

4 Who, in 1889, invented the pneumatic tyre?   D . . . . .

5 The wide lower tidal part of a river.   E . . . . . .

6 Semi-tropical wading bird. F . . . .

7 Norwegian composer of *Peer Gynt*. G . . . .

8 Author of *Far From The Madding Crowd*. H . . . .

9 The period for hatching out of eggs. I . . . .

10 A person who is registered as a dealer on the stock exchange. J . . . . .

11 Method of unarmed self-defence. K . . . . .

12 Scottish missionary who discovered the Victoria Falls. L . . . .

13 Where is the Ka'Ba? M . . . .

14 What word links park, debt and service? N . . . .

15 Woodwind musical instrument. O . . .

16 Vast treeless plains of South America. P . . . . .

17 City at the mouth of the St Lawrence River. Q . . . . .

18 Old instrument of torture. R . . .

19 Meaning of Latin phrase *compos mentis*. S . . .

20 The person making a will. T . . . .

21 Republic of East Africa. U . . . . .

22 Screen name of Rodolpho d'Antonguolla. V . . . .

23 A thin crisp biscuit. W . . . .

24 Musical instrument with 30–45 strings. Z . . . . .

SIXTEEN

1 Long wooden horn used by herdsmen.   A . . . .

2 Broom made of twigs.   B . . . .

3 Merry-go-round.   C . . . .

4 Washerman.   D . . . .

5 Meet by chance.   E . . . .

6 Cultivated large nut.   F . . . . . .

7 Shackle.   G . . .

8 Suicide by disembowelment.   H . . .-. . . .

9 Drunken person.   I . . . .

10 Founder of christianity   J . . . .

11 Australian marsupial.   K . . . .

12 Set free.   L . . . .

13 Masked ball.   M . . . .

14 Loop with running knot.   N . . . .

15 Enclosure with fruit trees.   O . . . . . .

16 Straw mattress.   P . . . .

17 Insubstantial argument.   Q . . . . .

18 Reddish brown.   R . . . . .

19 Petty or noisy quarrel.   S . . . .

20 Dinner jacket.   T . . . . .

21 Emit audibly.   U . . . .

22 Of spring.   V . . . . .

23 Swing round and round.   W . . . .

24 City in northern England, Latin name Eboracum.   Y . . .

SEVENTEEN

1 North American Indian tribe.   A . . . . .

2 Instrument for measuring
pressure in the atmosphere.   B . . . .

3 Son of Venus.   C . . . .

4 What city occupies an oasis in
the Syrian desert?   D . . . .

5 What became independent on
28 February 1922?   E . . . .

6 Material used in soldering.   F . . .

7 American Civil War general
who became President in 1868.   G . . . .

8 What word means hinder and
basket?   H . . . . .

9 Under an assumed identity.   I . . . .

10 Burglar's short crowbar.   J . . . .

11 Scottish pirate hanged in
1701.   K . . .

12 Painter of 'The Virgin of the
Rocks'.   L . . . .

13 Who wrote of *Quinquireme of
Nineveh from distant ophir*?   M . . . .

14 Lake in Scotland which forms
part of the Caledonian Canal.   N . . .

15 Aquatic carnivorous
mammal.   O . . . .

16 Who defended Antonio
against Shylock?   P . . . . .

17 What society of friends was
founded by George Fox (1624–
1691)?   Q . . . . . .

18 Artificial silk.   R . . . .

19   Small food-fish of the herring family.   S . . . .

20   Smallest type of British wild duck.   T . . .

21   All space and all matter contained in space.   U . . . .

22   Small blood-sucking bat of Central and South America.   V . . . . . .

23   Village in Belgium, scene of a British military victory in 1815.   W . . . .

24   Courgette.   Z . . . .

EIGHTEEN

1   Long iron-tipped staff used in mountain climbing.   A . . . .

2   Rail or coping on parapet.   B . . . .

3   Entertainment in restaurant.   C . . . . . .

4   Lie still.   D . . . .

5   Fit to be eaten.   E . . . . .

6   Face of building towards the street.   F . . . . .

7   Lightly seasoned stew of meat and vegetable.   G . . . . . .

8   Haggard or ill-tempered woman.   H . . . . . .

9   Reconstructed picture of a person.   I . . . .

10   Hard, green, blue or white stone.   J . . .

11   Soldier's canvas bag.   K . . . .

12   Articles needed for new born baby.   L . . . . . .

13 Pliable sheathlike connective tissue. M . . . .

14 Feeling of sickness. N . . . . .

15 Great quantity. O . . . . .

16 Vertical fence of wood. P . . . . .

17 External angle of building. Q . . . .

18 Smelling or tasting of stale fat. R . . . . .

19 Broad brimmed hat of felt or straw. S . . . .

20 Claw of bird of prey. T . . . .

21 Coincided in pitch. U . . . . .

22 Variety entertainment. V . . . .

23 Woman practising sorcery. W . . . .

24 Musical instrument of flat wooden bars. X . . . .

NINETEEN

1 Roman slave who removed a thorn from a lion's paw. A . . . .

2 Alloy containing 50 to 70 per cent copper. B . . . .

3 What kind of 'chappie' was Max Miller? C . . . . .

4 Town in Greece where stood the Temple of Apollo. D . . . . .

5 National park and moorland in Devon and Somerset. E . . . . .

6 King of Egypt exiled in 1952. F . . . . .

7 Capital of Guyana. G . . . .

8 Vehicle developed by Sir Christopher Cockerell. H . . . .

9 A furnace for burning things. I . . . .

10 The better side of a R. L. Stevenson character. J . . . . .

11 Title of former emperors of Germany and Austria. K . . . . .

12 A maze of winding passages. L . . . .

13 Writer of *Paradise Lost* and *Paradise Regained*. M . . . . .

14 Small square of table linen or paper. N . . . . .

15 Where would you find Columbus and Cleveland? O . . .

16 Black and white in patches. P . . . . . .

17 Twenty-four sheets of paper. Q . . . .

18 What river rises in the Swiss Alps and ends in a delta in Holland? R . . . .

19 Who practised his golf shots during a moonwalk in February 1971? S . . . . . .

20 A ballet dancer's short skirt. T . . .

21 What word connects take, write and stand? U . . . .

22 Rate of change of position. V . . . .

23 Actor whose real name was Marion Michael Morrison. W . . . .

24 A line or road with sharp angles. Z . . . . .

TWENTY

---

1 Public slaughterhouse. A . . . .

2 Noisy publicity. B . . . . . .

3 Pyramid of rough stones. C . . . .

4 Short-legged long-bodied breed of dog. D . . . .

5 Wooden frame to support blackboard. E . . . .

6 Young bird. F . . . .

7 The son of Lancelot. G . . . . .

8 American tree of the walnut family. H . . . . . .

9 Body of Bantu warriors. I . . .

10 Person who brings bad luck. J . . . .

11 Blood relationship. K . . . . . .

12 Short-horned edible grasshoppers. L . . . . . .

13 World wide. M . . . . . .

14 Wind. N . . . . .-. . . . .

15 Swift running flightless bird. O . . . . .

16 Paste of meat. P . . .

17 Hunchback of Notre Dame. Q . . . .

18 Circular, round. R . . . . .

19 Small piece cut off. S . . . . . .

20 Fine silk. T . . . .

21 Father's or mother's brother. U . . . .

22 Which saint's day is celebrated in February? V . . . .

23 Dance in triple time. W . . . .

24 Figure 0 or zilch. Z . . .

TWENTY-ONE

1 Which goddess sprang full grown from the sea? A . . . .

2   Comic treatment of a dignified subject. B . . . .

3   On which river is the Boulder Dam? C . . . .

4   Government of the people, by the people, for the people. D . . . .

5   To register for service. E . . . . .

6   A receiver of stolen goods. F . . . .

7   Prickly shrub with yellow flowers. G . . . .

8   A sea-fish of the cod family. H . . . . . .

9   To take legal possession. I . . . . . .

10   Careless pedestrian who is a hazard to motorists. J . . . .

11   Zambian statesman elected president (1964) at independence. K . . . . .

12   What kind of creature is a basilisk? L . . . . .

13   What gas causes danger in coal-mines? M . . . . . .

14   Mohammedan prince or noble. N . . . . .

15   Excess of body fat usually the result of over-eating. O . . . . . .

16   North American Indian tribe. P . . . . .

17   Mercury. Q . . . .

18   Which people first used central heating? R . . . . .

19   River over which Charon ferried the dead. S . . .

20   American president who succeeded F. D. Roosevelt. T . . . . .

21   Legendary horse-like animal. U . . . . . .

26

22 What city's name in Chile literally translated means 'vale of paradise'?   V . . . .

23 Surname of 1st Duke of Wellington.   W . . . .

24 Veil worn by Mohammedan women.   Y . . . . . .

TWENTY-TWO

1 What continent extends the same distance both north and south of the equator?   A . . . . .

2 Second Greek letter.   B . . .

3 Large flightless bird.   C . . . .

4 Mathematical system which uses multiples of ten.   D . . . . . .

5 Full of keen desire.   E . . . .

6 Flaming torch.   F . . . .

7 Bird's second stomach for grinding food.   G . . . . . .

8 One who announces another's approach.   H . . . .

9 To drink, especially alcoholic liquor.   I . . . . .

10 Body of persons sworn to render verdict.   J . . .

11 Tomato sauce.   K . . . . . .

12 Herbaceous plant.   L . . . . . .

13 Experienced and trusted advisor.   M . . . . .

14 Inexperienced person.   N . . . . . .

15 Furred aquatic mammal.   O . . . .

16	Piece of land for cattle.	P . . . . . .
17	Quasi-autonomous national government organization.	Q . . . . .
18	Cuban Negro dance.	R . . . .
19	Tranquil, composed, settled.	S . . . . .
20	Hillock of grass.	T . . . . .
21	Petticoat.	U . . . .
22	Depart hurriedly.	V . . . . . .
23	Marriage ceremony.	W . . . . . .
24	Striped ass-like animal.	Z . . . .

TWENTY-THREE

1	Small mountainous country in the Balkans.	A . . . . . .
2	City built in 7th Century BC by King Nebuchadnezzar.	B . . . .
3	Largest island of the West Indies.	C . . .
4	Machine for generating electric current.	D . . . . .
5	Sea-ducks sought after for their fine down.	E . . . .
6	What word connects man, citizen and ship.	F . . . . .
7	Stage name of Frances Gumm.	G . . . . . .
8	Metric unit of area equal to 10,000 square metres.	H . . . . . .
9	To solicit for immoral purposes.	I . . . .
10	Money pool in card games.	J . . . . . .
11	Japanese suicide pilots.	K . . . .

12 American poet, writer of *The Wreck of the Hesperus*.　　　L . . . .

13 Austrian composer of *Don Giovanni*.　　　M . . . . .

14 What was discovered by John Cabot on 24 June 1497?　　　N . . . .

15 A solid bounded by eight plane faces.　　　O . . . .

16 What writing material is made by dressing the skins of animals?　　　P . . . .

17 Wet muddy ground.　　　Q . . . .

18 Currency unit of India.　　　R . . . . .

19 Broad, treeless plains in South Russia.　　　S . . . . . .

20 The tinkling sound of bells.　　　T . . . .

21 Too deep to be understood.　　　U . . . .

22 What kind of creatures are fish, reptiles and birds?　　　V . . . .

23 British author of *Kipps*.　　　W . . . .

24 German inventor who built first motor-driven airship.　　　Z . . . .

TWENTY-FOUR

1 Kind of llama with long woolly hair.　　　A . . . . .

2 Low basin for washing.　　　B . . . .

3 The whole lot.　　　C . . . .

4 Party where records are played.　　　D . . . .

5 Become void.　　　E . . . . .

6 Religious festival in Spain. F . . . . .

7 Swedish actress, star of *Anna Karenina* (1935). G . . . . .

8 Estate with dwelling house in Spain. H . . . .

9 Gum producing sweet smell when burned. I . . . . . .

10 Punishment for defaulters in the army J . . . . . .

11 Work into dough. K . . . .

12 Tough fibrous tissue binding bones together. L . . . .

13 Collection of wild animals in captivity. M . . . .

14 The capital of Tennessee. N . . . .

15 Cushioned seat. O . . . . . .

16 Small parrot. P . . . .

17 Ballroom dance Q . . . .

18 Appearance of country people. R . . . . .

19 Holiness of life. S . . . .

20 Outburst of bad temper. T . . . . . .

21 Combed up and arranged in a pile on the head. U . . . . . .

22 Pasta made in long slender threads. V . . . .

23 Flat purse for carrying bank notes. W . . . . .

24 Slow-growing evergreen coniferous tree. Y . .

TWENTY-FIVE

1   Form of speech, e.g. 'big black block'.   A . . . .

2   Prison fortress in Paris stormed by a mob on 14 July 1789.   B . . . .

3   International phonetic code name for 'c'.   C . . . . . .

4   What feature do the Nile, Ganges, Volga and Mississippi rivers, have?   D . . . . .

5   Inventor of gramophone and incandescent electric lamp.   E . . . . .

6   Oscillations measured in cycles per second.   F . . . .

7   Performance of athletic exercises.   G . . . .

8   What word connects a country and a New Zealand prime minister? H . . . . . .

9   Natural resistance of an organism to specific infections.   I . . . .

10   Author of *Three Men in a Boat*.   J . . . . .

11   Loose breeches gathered in at the knee.   K . . . .

12   Bolshevist leader, real name Vladim Ilich Ulianoff.   L . . . .

13   King of Scotland slain by Malcolm Canmore, Duncan's son, in 1056.   M . . . . . .

14   Whose remains repose in the Hôtel des Invalides at Paris?   N . . . . . .

15   Not perpendicular.   O . . . . . .

31

16 Currency unit of Spain.   P . . . . .

17 A case for arrows.   Q . . . . .

18 What is *sequoia sempervirens*,
the largest of its species, better
known as?   R . . . . . .

19 Capital of Bulgaria.   S . . . .

20 African fly which spreads
diseases by its bite.   T . . . . .

21 Institute of highest level of
education.   U . . . .

22 In Shakespeare's play of 1594
where did two gentleman hail
from?   V . . . . .

23 Roman road (street) which
ran from Dover to Chester.   W . . . . . .

24 In cricket, a ball pitching just
under the bat.   Y . . . . .

TWENTY-SIX

1 One who calculates insurance
risk.   A . . . . . .

2 Game for two people played
with dice and counters on a
board.   B . . . .

3 Light clear red.   C . . . . .

4 Worthless verse.   D . . . .

5 Approximate judgement.   E . . . .

6 Spanish gypsy style of song
and dance.   F . . . .

7 Projecting waterspout.   G . . . .

8 Mixture of sand and gravel.   H . . . . .

32

9	Language of the people.	I . . . .
10	Sharp sudden pull.	J . . .
11	Small falcon.	K . . . . . .
12	Glaringly colourful.	L . . . .
13	Province of Canada.	M . . . .
14	Stupid person.	N . . . .
15	The largest bird.	O . . . . . .
16	Passage or section of book.	P . . . .
17	The first Sunday in Lent.	Q . . . .
18	Chess piece which looks like a castle.	R . . .
19	Sparkle and twinkle.	S . . . .
20	Commonplace.	T . . . .
21	The mountains separating Europe from Asia.	U . . . .
22	Oscillate.	V . . . .
23	Inflammation near nail on finger.	W . . . . . .
24	Old name for Tokyo.	Y . . .

TWENTY-SEVEN

1	Musical term 'slowish'.	A . . . . . .
2	Science which deals with life in all its forms.	B . . . . . .
3	What ancient creature was half a horse?	C . . . . . .
4	Who is the Earl of Beaconsfield (1804–81) better known as?	D . . . .
5	Pen name of Mary Ann Evans 19th-Century novelist.	E . . . .

6 Capital of Sierra Leone. F . . . .

7 Universal force of attraction between bodies. G . . . .

8 Strait off Iran connecting Persian Gulf with Gulf of Oman H . . . . .

9 What word connects the eye with a Greek goddess? I . . .

10 Historic capital of Palestine. J . . . .

11 Straight-faced American silent film comedian. K . . . . .

12 Quarter day in Scotland, 1st August. L . . . . .

13 What kind of creatures are oysters and snails? M . . . .

14 Who fell in love with his own reflected image? N . . . .

15 Setting to music of a religious theme. O . . . .

16 Who wrote *The Good Companions*? P . . . .

17 An oddity of character or behaviour. Q . . . .

18 What English surname means 'red-haired'? R . . . . . .

19 Figure of speech, e.g. 'let us drink to the queer old dean'. S . . . .

20 Brass musical instrument formally called sackbut. T . . . .

21 Without like or equal. U . . . . .

22 International phonetic code name for 'v'. V . . . . .

23 Writer of *Compleat Angler*. W . . . . .

24 Of what country is Sana the capital? Y . . . .

34

1	Method of pricking skin with needle to cure illness.	A . . . .
2	Negligible amount.	B . . . .
3	Collarbone.	C . . . .
4	Mythical monster-like reptile.	D . . . . .
5	Moving staircase.	E . . . .
6	Wreckage found floating.	F . . . . . .
7	Method of strangulation.	G . . . . . .
8	The masses.	H . . . .
9	Sharp-edged cutting teeth.	I . . . .
10	Large carnivorous spotted feline.	J . . . . .
11	Furnace for baking bricks.	K . . .
12	Christian period of fasting.	L . . .
13	Bone of the foot.	M . . . .
14	Short story.	N . . . .
15	Capital of Norway.	O . . .
16	Dish made in Italy from dried flour paste.	P . . . .
17	Inflammation of the throat.	Q . . . . .
18	Tumbledown, crazy, rickety.	R . . . .
19	Brief general summary.	S . . . .
20	Large black spider.	T . . . .
21	Imaginary island of perfection.	U . . . . .
22	Open country.	V . . . .
23	Smallest British bird.	W . . .
24	Serbo-Croatian language.	Y . . . .

TWENTY-NINE

1   Person with unnaturally white skin and hair, and pink eyes.

A l b i n o

2   Place in Surrey, centre for British rifle-shooting competitions.

B . . . . .

3   Dried and salted roe of sturgeon.

C a v i a r e

4   Game of 28 bones.

D . . . .

5   Language first published in 1887 by Dr Louis Zamenhof.

E s p e r a n t o

6   American statesman and scientist who had a somewhat enlightening experience.

F r a n k l i n

7   Who wrote *Ruddigore*?

G i l b e r t

8   Amorphous, black organic matter in soil.

H . . . .

9   Any positive or negative whole number including zero.

I n t e g e r

10   City of South Transvaal, South Africa.

J o h a n n e s b u r g

11   Jewish communal agricultural settlement in Israel.

K i b b u t z

12   Common name for the gas nitrous oxide.

L . . . .

13   Capital of Liberia.

M . . . .

14   What river forms the outlet to four of North America's great lakes?

N i a g a r a

15   International phonetic code name for 'o'.

O . . . .

16   Plants which continue to flower year after year.

P e r e n n i a l s .

17   A shallow, usually wooden, drinking cup.

Q . . . . .

18 Syncopated music. R ythmic

19 A triangle with no two sides equal. S . . . . . .

20 Scottish civil engineer who built the Caledonian Canal. T . . . . . .

21 A student who has not taken his first degree. U ndergraduate

22 Virgin priestesses of ancient Rome. V estals

23 A craving for change of place and thirst for travel. W anderlust

24 Youngest of the five Marx brothers. Z eppo

THIRTY

1 With hands on hips and elbows turned outwards. A . . . . .

2 Small bar or restaurant. B istro

3 Large stadium. C . . . .

4 Athletic contest comprising ten events. D ecathlon

5 Person having special skills. E . . . . .

6 Whipping fanatics of the 14th century. F lagelators

7 Smooth durable twill woven cloth of worsted cotton. G . . . .

8 Layer of the ionosphere 60–70 miles high. H . . . .

9 Chimney corner. I . . . .-. . . .

10 Roman god of doors and gates. J anus

11 Dust coloured uniform. K haki

12 Manservant. L . . . . .

13   Straps on a horse to prevent rearing.   M . . . .

14   Stupid person.   N . . . . .

15   What flavour is Grand Marnier?   O range

16   Picture of landscape.   P . . . .

17   Lump of tobacco.   Q . . .

18   Flat fish allied to shark.   R . .

19   Close investigation.   S . . . .

20   Feeble talk.   T . . . . . .

21   Which acid is found in urine?   U . . .

22   Group of birds.   V . . . . .

23   Which country was known as Cambria?   W ales

24   Earnestness.   Z eal

THIRTY-ONE

1   Salt or soil deposited by running water.   A . . . .

2   Wild ox of North American origin.   B ison

3   The largest single family of succulents.   C . . . .

4   Regions of calm sea near the Equator.   D oldrums

5   Meaning of Latin phrase *in toto*.   E . . . .

6   Dutch author of *The Diary of a Young Girl* (1947).   F rank

7   Type of carnivorous brown bear *Ursus horribilis*.   G rizzly

38

8 What was the only thing which failed to escape from Pandora's box?

H . . .

9 Want of steadiness.

I . . . .

10 Combat sport developed in Japan.

J *udo*

11 Capital of Afghanistan.

K *abul*

12 Light machine gun.

L . . . .

13 What was under siege from 12 Oct 1899 to 17 May 1900?

M *afeking*

14 Inventor of dynamite and gelignite.

N . . . .

15 Branch of zoology dealing with birds.

O *rnothology*

16 Alloy of four parts tin to one part lead.

P *enter*

17 Pleasantly old-fashioned.

Q *uaint*

18 A quick return thrust after a parry.

R . . . . . .

19 Sultan of Syria who captured Jerusalem in 1187.

S *aladin*

20 What was captained by Edward J. Smith.

T *itanic*

21 An insurer.

U *nderwriter*

22 What word connects cross and falls.

V . . . .

23 International phonetic code name for 'w'.

W *hisky*

24 The point of the celestial sphere directly above the observer.

Z *enith*

THIRTY-TWO

1 Tool for cutting away surface of wood.

A . . .

2 Shot gun with large bore.

B lunderbess

3 Spanish gentleman.

C . . . .

4 Lateen-rigged Arabian sea ship.

D how

5 Dash.

E . . .

6 Plant from which digitalis can be obtained.

F . . . .

7 Chess opening involving sacrifice.

G . . . . .

8 Famous escapologist 1874–1926.

H oudini

9 Egyptian goddess of fertility.

I sis

10 Complaint which turns the skin yellow.

J aundice

11 Area of Canada near Alaska, home of the gold rush.

K . . . .

12 Salt water separated from the sea by low sandbank.

L agoon

13 Greek dish of mincemeat, aubergines, eggs, etc.

M oussaka

14 Noodle or simpleton.

N . . . .

15 Musical instrument called a sweet potato.

O . . . . . .

16 German armoured troops.

P anzers

17 Person given to gossip.

Q . . . .

18 Poisonous American snake.

R attlesnake

19 Game played on ship's deck.

S . . . . .-. . .

20 Lattice of wood for fence.

T rellis

21 Group of ravens.

U . . . .

40

22 Great waterfall on the Zambesi.

V *ictoria*

23 Group of swans.

W . . . .

24 To move quickly.

Z . . .

THIRTY-THREE

1 Small fish, allied to the herring.

A *nchovy*

2 Science of plant life.

B *otany*

3 Anthropoid ape found in Equatorial Africa.

C *himpanzee*

4 Whose pen name was Boz?

D *ickens*

5 Very hard dark wood.

E *bony*

6 What word connects a Dutchman, a fox and a lemur?

F . . . . .

7 Leading 18th-century actor, buried in Westminster Abbey.

G *arrick*

8 Official report of parliamentary proceedings.

H . . . . . .

9 Title given to the best cavalry troops of Oliver Cromwell.

I *ronsides*

10 A bringer of bad luck.

J . . .

11 Seaport and peninsula of Hong Kong.

K *owloon*

12 Long-tailed crustacean.

L . . . . . .

13 White floury coating on the leaves and shoots of plants.

M . . . . .

14 SI unit of force.

N *ewton*

15 All powerful.

O *mnipotent*

16 Opposition to the use of armed force.

P *acifism*

41

17 A hunted animal. Q *Harry*

18 Landlord exposed in 1963 for charging extortionate rent for slum conditions. R . . . . . .

19 Mountainous Italian island south of Corsica. S *ardinia*

20 Poet-musician of Middle Ages in southern France. T *roubadour*

21 Tense or nervous. U . . . . . .

22 Region and former kingdom of eastern Spain. V *alencia*

23 English novelist, works include *Brideshead Revisited* (1945). W *augh*

24 International phonetic code name for 'y'. Y . . . . .

THIRTY-FOUR

1 Pineapple. A *nanas*
2 Small shop selling clothes. B *outique*
3 Collusion. C . . . . . .
4 Person with morbid craving for liquor. D *ipsomaniac*
5 Words inscribed on tomb. E *pitaph*
6 Of iron. F *errous*
7 Small African or Asian antelope. G *azelle*
8 Pert girl. H . . . .
9 State of north-west USA. I *daho*
10 Young kangaroo. J *oey*
11 Indonesian dagger. K . . . .

12 Close-fitting one-piece garment.　L . . . . . .

13 Lowest fore and aft sail of full-rigged ship.　M . . . . .

14 Harmful.　N oxious

15 Mollusc with eight suckered arms.　O ctopus

16 Large furniture van.　P . . . .

17 Open tart with filling.　Q uiche

18 Small stream.　R . . .

19 Composition for full orchestra.　S ymphony

20 Vacuum flask.　T . . . . . .

21 Where is Montevideo?　U ruguay

22 Scandinavian trader and pirate.　V iking

23 Sharpen on stone.　W het

24 Expression of delight.　Y ippee

THIRTY-FIVE

1 Who did Anna Anderson claim to be?　A nastasia

2 Who was Rafael Sabatini's famous pirate captain?　B . . . .

3 Home of Sir Winston Churchill for 40 years.　C . . . .

4 Who voyaged for five years round the world in HMS Beagle?　D arwin

5 The study of organisms in relation to the environment.　E cology

6 One who shoes horses.　F . . . . . .

43

7 Wheel mounted so that it is free to rotate about any axis.

G *Gyroscope*

8 Former royal family of Austria.

H *Hapsburgs*

9 Norwegian dramatist author of *Hedda Gabler*.

I *Ibsen*

10 Large Indonesian island.

J *Java*

11 Ash obtained by burning seaweed.

K . . .

12 Order of insects, comprising moths and butterflies.

L . . . .

13 Former name of Iraq.

M *Mesopotamia*

14 Small mug or wooden cup.

N *Noggin*

15 The science of light and vision.

O *Optics*

16 What 19th-century politician introduced a line on ships to prevent overloading?

P . . . .

17 A trembling of the voice.

Q *Wavper*

18 Small pieces of noodle paste with savoury filling.

R *ravioli*

19 Apparatus to detect earth tremors.

S *seismograph*

20 Largest island of the Lesser Antilles of the West Indies.

T *Trinidad*

21 Fruit which is a cross between the grapefruit and tangerine.

U . . .

22 Capital of Malta.

V . . . .

23 What is the name of the Royal Horticultural Society Gardens near Ripley in Surrey?

W . . . . .

24 Gaseous element present in the atmosphere in minute quantities.

X . . . .

44

THIRTY-SIX

1   Watch chain with crossbar.   A . . . . .

2   Cylinder from which thread is
unwound.   B . . . . .

3   Large watertight chamber.   C . . . . .

4   Bulging narrow-necked bottle.   D . . . . . .

5   Ooze out.   E . . . .

6   Gambling card game.   F . . .

7   Drawing or writing on walls.   G r a f f i t i

8   Group of six.   H . . . .

9   The Holm Oak.   I . . .

10 Species of narcissus.   J . . . . . .

11 Crest of hill.   K . . .

12 Golf club.   L . . . . .

13 Of mice.   M . . . . .

14 Marriageable.   N . . . . .

15 Burdensome.   O n e r o u s

16 Knee cap.   P . . . . . .

17 A landing place   Q u a g

18 Name for the fox.   R e g n a r d

19 Run away.   S . . . .

20 Trunk of human.   T o r s o

21 Soft substance used as an
ointment.   U . . . . . .

22 Open grassland of South
Africa.   V e l d t

23 Head-covering worn by
nuns.   W i m p l e

24 Hindu system of meditation.   Y o g a

THIRTY-SEVEN

1 What fortress-palace is built in the hills near Granada in Spain?

A lhambra

2 American composer-conductor whose works include *West Side Story*.

B ernstein

3 Circular violent storm.

C yclone

4 The goddess of hunting and twin sister of Apollo.

D iana

5 Fit or worthy to be chosen.

E ligible

6 Small yellowish-brown deer.

F . . . . .

7 American film director-producer whose best-known film is *Birth of a Nation* (1915).

G . . . .

8 British inventor of the spinning jenny.

H . . . .

9 Not liable to sin.

I . . . .

10 Plant with fragrant yellow, red or white flowers.

J . . . . . .

11 Scottish religious reformer.

K nox

12 Who said 'The ballot is stronger than the bullet'?

L incoln

13 What game was invented by Charles Darrow in 1933?

M onopoly

14 Smooth variety of peach.

N ectarine

15 Sheep-like.

O . . . .

16 Legendary bird which after 500 years builds its own funeral pyre.

P hoenix

17 Doubtful.

Q uestionable

18 Who rode from Charlestown to Lexington in 1775?

R evere

46

19   Where are Palermo and Messina?   S *icily*

20   Who wrote the poem *The Brook*?   T *ennyson*

21   British political party formed 1886 to maintain parliamentary union of Britain and Ireland.   U *nionist*

22   White wine flavoured with aromatic herbs.   V . . . .

23   The ridge between the shoulder-bones of a horse.   W *ithers*

24   Language which is a compound of Hebrew and German.   Y *iddish*

THIRTY-EIGHT

1   Musical movement in brisk time.   A *llegro*

2   Card game for two.   B . . . . . .

3   Shrill sounding insect.   C *riket*

4   Airship.   D . . . .

5   Bringing into state of confusion.   E . . . .

6   Of public revenue.   F *iscal*

7   Evening twilight.   G . . . .

8   Foul breath.   H . . . .

9   Sloping type in printing.   I . . . . .

10   Simpleton.   J . . . . . .

11   Spirit distilled from wild cherries.   K . . . . .

12   Rope for tethering horses.   L . . . . .

13 Muslim priest.   M . . . . .

14 Japan.   N *ippon*

15 Of the eye.   O *ptic*

16 Inner court open to the sky.   P . . . .

17 The hollow stem of a feather.   Q *uill*

18 Rose-coloured.   R . . . . . .

19 Vertical strut.   S . . . .

20 Fine sword blade.   T . . . . .

21 Not immediately.   U . . . .

22 Convert into glass.   V . . . . . .

23 Guardian's care.   W *ardship*

24 Whist or bridge hand with no
card above a nine.   Y . . . .

THIRTY-NINE

1 Who said that the upward
thrust exerted on a body immersed
in fluid equals the weight of fluid
displaced?   A *rchemedes*

2 What herb is a popular
seasoning for minestrone soup?   B *asil*

3 Underground burial places.   C *atacombs*

4 Minstrel song which became
the battle hymn of the confederacy
during the Civil War.   D *ixie*

5 Mountain with notorious
north face.   E . . . .

6 The thigh-bone.   F . . . .

7 Author of *The Decline and Fall
of the Roman Empire*.   G *ibbon*

48

8   Carthaginian soldier defeated by Scipio at Zama in 202 BC.

H annibal

9   Hint or intimation.

I . . . . . .

10   Casual trousers.

J eans

11   Writer of *Westward Ho!*.

K . . . . . .

12   Musical instrument similar to the harp.

L yre

13   What synthetic dye produced in 1859 was named after a battle?

M . . . . . .

14   Prophetic French astrologer and physician.

N ostradamus

15   Winner of four track and field gold medals in 1936 Olympics.

O wens

16   Small, high-pitched sounding flute.

P iccolo

17   State of N E Australia.

Q ueensland

18   Bordering on the improper.

R isque

19   King of Israel after his father, David.

S olomon

20   British novelist who wrote *Vanity Fair*.

T hackery .

21   Awkward and ungraceful in manners.

U ncouth

22   Italian composer whose works include *The Four Seasons*.

V ivaldi

23   What are colt's-foot, ragwort and toad flax?

W ildflowers

24   National park which contains the highest waterfall in North America.

Y . . . .

FORTY

1 Self possession.   A . . . . .

2 Russian wolf hound.   B . . . . .

3 Apple brandy.   C . . . . . .

4 Crane on board ship.   D . . . .

5 Fairness.   E quity

6 Dish of flavoured melted cheese.   F ondue

7 Herdsman in South America.   G aucho

8 Election proceedings.   H ustings

9 Of fire.   I gneous

10 Sweet drink.   J . . . .

11 Small seagull-type bird.   K . . . . . .

12 Brief, concise.   L . . . . . .

13 Gruesome.   M . . . . . .

14 Of weddings.   N uptual

15 Not transmitting light.   O . . . . .

16 Pinkish-brown smooth nut.   P ecan

17 Hanging plaited hair.   Q . . . .

18 Dry white wine from Europe.   R iesling

19 Foolish person.   S . . . . . .

20 Group of three.   T . . . .

21 Shadow cast by earth.   U mbra

22 Short wooden wax match.   V . . . .

23 Leather loop worn around scout's neckerchief.   W oggle

24 Sixth Greek letter.   Z eta

FORTY-ONE

1 Chief hero of Homer's Iliad. A *chilles*

2 Palace which was the birthplace of Sir Winston Churchill. B *lenheim*

3 Genus of cone-bearing trees. C . . . . .

4 Who wrote a novel based upon the career of Alexander Selkirk? D . . . . .

5 A widespreading group of states. E . . . . .

6 How often does a Mohammedan pray each day? F *ive*

7 11th-century wife of Leofric of Mercia. G *odiva*

8 Decorative stitch in needlework. H . . . .

9 What is the correct name of the plant Busy Lizzy? I . . . .

10 Species of crow. J *ackdaw*

11 The central wedge of an arch. K *eystone*

12 A word-book or dictionary. L . . . . . .

13 Who first sailed round the world? M *agellan*

14 The study of the nerves. N . . . .

15 Great South American river which flows across Venezuela. O *rinoco*

16 On what horse did Gordon Richards win the Derby in 1953? P . . . .

17 A proportional share. Q . . . .

18 Currency unit of USSR. R *ouble*

51

19   Inflammation of eyelid, centring on one eyelash.   S . . .

20   Regions of semi-barren, marshy land near the Arctic Circle.   T . . . . .

21   Working in secret.   U . . . .

22   Russian city, formerly Stalingrad.   V olgograd

23   English novelist who created Bertie Wooster and Jeeves.   W odhouse

24   International phonetic code name for 'z'.   Z . . .

FORTY-TWO

1   Hinged flap on rear edge of aeroplane wing.   A . . . . . .

2   European fresh-water fish.   B . . . . .

3   Cooking room on a ship's deck.   C . . . . . .

4   Fold of loose skin hanging from neck of turkey.   D . . . . .

5   Error in printing.   E rratum

6   Of a son or daughter.   F . . . . .

7   Slide down steep slope.   G . . . . . .

8   Something between a discourse and a sermon.   H . . . . .

9   Short description of picturesque scene.   I . . . .

10   Long riding breeches.   J odhpurs

11   Cloth used to cover head.   K . . . .

12   Art of moving troops and equipment.   L . . . .

13 Appease.   M . . . . . .
14 Delicate difference.   N uance
15 The west.   O ccident
16 Smallness of quantity.   P . . . . . .
17 Four-sided open court.   Q uadrangle
18 Italian dish of rice with
stock.   R issoto
19 Shoulder blade.   S . . . . . .
20 Lottery.   T . . . . . .
21 Fleshy part of the soft palate.   U . . . .
22 Graduated scale.   V . . . . . .
23 Verbose but ignorant tale.   W . . . . . .
24 Science of animal structure.   Z oology

FORTY-THREE

1 Where is the temple which is
the centre of Sikh religion?   A mritsar

2 *Semperflorens* is a variety of
what plant?   B . . . . . .

3 Sixty-six feet.   C . . . .

4 An apparatus for lifting
weights.   D . . . . . .

5 Poetic name for Ireland.   E . . .

6 What are Hepplewhite and
Sheraton types of?   F urniture

7 Who painted the 'Blue Boy'?   G ainsbourgh.

8 French protestants of 16th and
17th centuries.   H uguenots.

9 Region of upper atmosphere.   I . . . .

10 A Chinese vessel.   J unk

11   American politician awarded Nobel Peace Prize in 1973.

K *issinger*

12   Elizabethan mansion and safari park near Warminster, Wiltshire.

L *onglect*

13   Originator of the doctrine of 'America for the Americans'.

M *onroe*

14   Where would you find Lincoln and Omaha?

N *ebraska*

15   Independent sultanate of south east Arabia.

O *man*

16   What did the ancient Egyptians write on?

P *apyrus*

17   To crush.

Q *uash*

18   From what is the Japanese drink sake made?

R *ice*

19   Currency unit of Austria.

S *chilling*

20   The art of shaping shrubs by cutting or pruning.

T . . . . . .

21   Science of sound vibrations higher than those normally audible to the human ear.

U *ltrasonics*

22   Six-a-side team game played on a rectangular court.

V *olleyball*

23   Who wrote *To a Skylark*?

W *ordsworth*

24   Persian king who defeated the Greeks at Thermopylae (480 BC).

X *erxes*

FORTY-FOUR

1   Young man of beauty named after sun god.

A *pollo*

2	Gambling card game.	B . . . . . .
3	Furnished with battlements.	C . . . .
4	Crown.	D i a d e m
5	Set forth in detail, explain.	E x p o u n d
6	Maker or seller of arrows.	F . . . . . .
7	Chin tuft like goat's beard.	G o a t e e
8	Game played on a board of 256 squares.	H a l m a
9	Ninth Greek letter.	I o t a
10	Gibberish.	J . . . . .
11	South African gold coin.	K r u g e r a n d
12	Dismal.	L u g u b r i o u s
13	Latin American dance like the rumba.	M . . . .
14	Parsimonious person.	N . . . . . .
15	American small nocturnal animal.	O . . . . . .
16	Schoolmaster.	P r i n c i p a l
17	Enthusiastic visionary.	Q . . . . . .
18	Debauchee, rake.	R o u é
19	Splinter of wood, bone, etc.	S . . . . . .
20	Gigantic.	T i t a n i c
21	Greasy, oily.	U . . . .
22	Able to fly.	V . . . . .
23	Small beetle found in stored grain.	W . . . . .
24	Horse between one and two years old.	Y . . . .

55

FORTY-FIVE

1 Class of vertebrate animals including frogs, toads and salamanders.

A *amphibia*

2 Capital of Colombia.

B *bogota*

3 A document which is supplementary to a will.

C . . . . . .

4 Country which lies on a peninsula dividing the North Sea from the Baltic.

D *denmark*

5 Act of driving evil spirits from a person or place.

E *exorcism*

6 Highest register of the male voice.

F *falsetto*

7 Protein extracted from bones with hot water.

G . . . .

8 International phonetic code name for 'h'.

H *hotel*

9 In ancient Rome, the 15th day of March, May, July and October and 13th of other months.

I *ides*

10 British commander of naval battle of Jutland, 1916.

J *jellicoe*

11 Large Australian bird with loud laughing cry.

K *kookaburra*

12 Gate at the entrance to a churchyard, usually with gabled roof.

L *lychgate*

13 Instrument for measurement of small lengths.

M . . . .

14 Type of golf club with wide face.

N . . . . . .

15 French composer of *Orpheus in the Underworld*.

O *offenbach*

56

16 Spanish conquistador; conqueror of Peru.

P *izzaro*

17 Ships officer who attends to supplies.

Q . . . .

18 A circular shaped knot of ribbon.

R *osseta*

19 Emblem found on Sumarian seals as early as 2850 BC.

S . . . .

20 Small bird of the gull family.

T . . .

21 Belonging to a city.

U *rban*

22 Travelling bag, usually leather, opening at the side.

V *alise*

23 A wizard.

W *arlock*

24 Second city of Yugoslavia.

Z *agreb*

FORTY-SIX

1 Alcoholic drink as appetiser.

A *peritif*

2 Child.

B *bairn*

3 Alligator.

C *ayman*

4 Betrayer of Samson.

D *elilah*

5 Inspire with love.

E *namour*

6 Part of horse's leg where tuft of hair grows.

F *etlock*

7 Connoisseur of table delicacies.

G . . . . . .

8 Scottish new year.

H *ogmanay*

9 Ignorant person.

I *gnoramus*

10 Where is St Helier?

J *ersey*

11 Coarse hair in wool.

K . . .

12 Pasta in wide sheet form.

L *asagne*

57

13	Short sightedness.	M . . . . .
14	Dreamy musical piece.	N . . . .
15	Size of book or page.	O . . . . .
16	Wooden patterned flooring.	P arquay
17	Quarter of a circle's circumference.	Q uadrant
18	Light two-wheeled hooded vehicle pulled along by coolie.	R icksahw
19	Small boat used in the Far East.	S ampan
20	Slightly drunk.	T . . . . .
21	Courteous.	U rbane
22	Wart.	V . . . . . .
23	Vagabond	W astrel
24	Stimulating flavour.	Z est

FORTY-SEVEN

1	Disbelief in the existence of a supreme being.	A theist
2	Which Dickens character said 'Oliver Twist has asked for more!'?	B . . . . .
3	Flesh-eating mammals.	C arnivours
4	The male of the honey-bee.	D rone
5	Swampy region of Florida, USA.	E verglades
6	Doctrine that everything which occurs is predetermined.	F atalism
7	German brothers and collectors of fairy stories.	G rimm

8   What word connects land, light and strong? H ead

9   The loss of one's good name leading to public disgrace. I . . . . . .

10   English judge notoriously harsh at the 'Bloody Assizes' in 1685. J effries

11   German canal 61 miles in length from North Sea to Baltic. K iel

12   Small burrowing rodent related to the vole. L . . . . . .

13   Which Gorgon was slain by Perseus? M edusa

14   Point directly opposite the zenith. N . . . .

15   Drug made from poppy seeds. O pium

16   Pianist; Prime Minister of Poland in 1919. P . . . .

17   Theory in physics to explain the discontinuous nature of energy within the atom. Q uantum

18   Sculptor of 'The Burghers of Calais'. R odin

19   In which sport do they compete for the Viyella Cup? S ailing

20   French national flag. T ricolour

21   Resembling a bear. U . . . . .

22   Building containing a cycle-racing track. V . . . .

23   Austrian diplomat and former UN secretary-general. W aldheim

24   African river which flows via the Victoria Falls and Kariba Dam. Z ambesi

FORTY-EIGHT

1 Arched or domed roof in church.

A *pse*

2 Scale of wind speed.

B . . . .

3 Like a goat.

C . . . . . .

4 Loin cloth worn by male Hindu.

D . . . .

5 Take woman in marriage.

E . . . . . .

6 Vault of the heavens with its clouds and stars.

F *irnament*

7 Bend the knee.

G *genuflect*

8 Armed foot soldier in ancient Greece.

H . . . . . .

9 Showing colours like those of the rainbow.

I . . . .

10 Dish of sweetened and flavoured curds.

J . . . . .

11 Chinese custom of absolute submission.

K . . . . .

12 Musical movement in slow time.

L . . . . .

13 Dunghill.

M *mixen*

14 Of the night.

N *nocturnal*

15 Composition for eight voices.

O *ctet*

16 Of shepherds.

P *astorel*

17 A million raised to the fourth power.

Q *Madrillion*

18 Rose garden.

R . . . .

19 Grassy plain with few or no trees.

S *avannah*

20 Ringing in the ears.

T . . . .

21 Amount by which a cask falls short of being full.

U . . . . .

60

22 Of the palm or sole. V . . . .

23 Ill tempered. W . . . . . .

24 Fox hunter's halloo. Y *oiks*

FORTY-NINE

1   Venue of America's annual Masters Golf Championship. A . . . . . .

2   Who did Lady Caroline Lamb describe as 'mad, bad and dangerous to know'? B *yron*

3   Founder of the Holy Roman Empire. C *harlemagne*

4   Word-blindness. D *yslexia*

5   The second book of the Old Testament. E *xodus*

6   What was the name of the 100–1 winner of the Grand National in 1967? F . . . .

7   Currency unit of the Netherlands. G *uilder*

8   Pompeii was one of two towns covered by the eruption of Vesuvius in AD 79. Which was the other? H *erculaneum*

9   What type of gases are neon, argon, krypton and xenon? I . . . .

10 Queen of the Netherlands from 1948–80. J *uliana*

11 Iranian Muslim religious leader. K *homeini*

12 Plant with purple flower grown as fodder. L . . . . . .

13 Person officially appointed to administer the law. M *agistrate*

61

14 Inflammable petroleum jelly.   N . . . . .

15 Large fish-feeding bird of
hawk family.   O *sprey*

16 Which chemical has the
symbol 'K'?   P . . . .

17 A repartee.   Q *uip*

18 Herb used to flavour roast
meats, stews, casseroles, etc.   R *osemary*

19 In Dickens' *Nicholas Nickelby*,
whose academy was Dotheboys
Hall?   S *queers*

20 Legislative body of the Isle of
Man.   T . . . . . .

21 Existence everywhere at the
same time.   U . . . .

22 Process of mixing sulphur
with rubber and applying heat.   V . . . .

23 A dam across a river.   W *eir*

24 Seaport of Japan on the south
east of Honshu Island.   Y *okohama*

FIFTY

1 Chemist.   A *pothecary*

2 Female spirit whose wail
portends evil or death.   B *anshee*

3 Two-wheeled hooded one-
horse chaise.   C . . . .

4 Crustacean with ten feet.   D *ecaped*

5 Preserve from decay.   E *mbalm*

6 Low soft felt hat.   F . . . . .

7 Lower part of horse's thighs.   G . . . . .

62

8 Bird with curved bill from Africa. H . . . . .

9 The keys of a piano. I . . . . . .

10 Locomotive crane. J . . . .

11 Male salmon in the spawning season. K . . . . .

12 Small marine animal. L . . . .

13 Situated in the middle. M . . . . .

14 One pound sterling. N ickey .

15 Loose fibre picked from old rope. O . . . .

16 Person without means of livelihood. P apper

17 Mineral form of silica. Q uartz

18 Machine for turning over soil. R . . . .

19 Very drunk. S ozzled

20 Of archery. T . . . .

21 Arrogant, snobbish. U ppity

22 The language of one's native country. V . . . .

23 Irresponsible. W . . . . .

24 Small three-masted vessel. X . . . .

FIFTY-ONE

1 Northern sea-bird. A . .

2 Author of *The Admirable Crichton*. B . . . . .

3 Who said '*Veni, vidi, vici*'? C aesar

4 What type of plant originated from Mexico and includes the varieties ball and collerette? D . . . . .

5 Large water jug with wide spout.

E . . .

6 Film actor who married Mary Pickford.

F . . . .

7 Small Central American country.

G *Guatamala*

8 Small insect-eating hibernating mammal.

H . . . .

9 School of painting amongst whose main exponents were Monet and Renoir.

I *mpressionist*

10 English architecture characteristic of the reign of James I.

J *acobean*

11 Where you will find Wichita and Topeka?

K *ansas*

12 Who sang 'A Little of What You Fancy Does You Good'?

L . . . .

13 Capital of ancient Egypt.

M . . . . . .

14 English industrialist who developed Morris Motors.

N *uffield*

15 The eighth part of a circle.

O . . . . .

16 John Rich (1692–1761) was the father of what form of entertainment?

P *antomine*

17 Most recent period of geological time.

Q . . . .

18 The mountain-ash.

R . . . .

19 Twelve-a-side stick and ball game played in Scottish highlands.

S . . . . .

20 In London, what are bush and cockpit?

T . . . .

21 The charging of excessive interest on a loan.

U *sury*

22 French writer whose real name was François Marie Arouet.

V oltaire

23 Town in Ireland famous for its glass industry.

W aterford

24 Chinese river, the longest in Asia.

Y angtze

FIFTY-TWO

1 Ideal rustic paradise.

A rcady

2 Temporary encampment without tents.

B ivouac

3 Guide versed in antiques.

C . . . . . .

4 Gypsy or itinerant tinker.

D . . . . .

5 Salad plant.

E . . . . .

6 High-pitched artificial voice.

F alsetto

7 Pregnant.

G . . . . .

8 Animal feeding on plants.

H erbivore

9 Mass of gold, silver, cast into a block.

I ngot

10 Lozenge of gelatin.

J . . . . .

11 Ruined.

K aput

12 Parrot-like Asian bird.

L . . .

13 Move or act listlessly.

M . . . . . .

14 Small tailed amphibian.

N ewt

15 Maker of a speech.

O rator

16 Small metal drinking vessel.

P annikin

17 Four-headed muscle at centre of thigh.

Q . . . .

18 Building with circular ground plan.

R otunda

19   Small African antelope.   S . . . .

20   Contraction of muscles of the
face.   T . .

21   British actor, and author of
Romanoff and Juliet (1956).   U . . . . . .

22   Thin semi-transparent cotton,
woollen or silken dress material.   V . . . .

23   Neglected child.   W *aif*

24   Young lamb or kid.   Y *earling*

FIFTY-THREE

1   The house plant *Hippeastrum*
is better known by what name?   A *maryllis*

2   Author of *Lorna Doone*.   B . . . .

3   In *The Winter's Tale* which
plant did Shakespeare describe as
'the fairest flowers o' the season'?   C . . . .

4   Capital of Bangladesh.   D *acca*

5   A feeling of weariness or
boredom.   E . . . .

6   In which theatre did John
Wilkes Booth assassinate President
Lincoln?   F . . . .

7   Type of sugar found in honey
and fruits.   G *lucose*

8   Astronomer who discovered
the planet Uranus.   H . . . .

9   Ancient Egyptian nature
goddess.   I *sis*

10   Mariner whose loss of an ear
caused a war between Britain and
Spain.   J . . . . . .

66

11   The SI unit of temperature.   K e l v i n

12   English artist, famous for his northern industrial landscapes.   L . . . .

13   Order of mammals including kangaroos and wallabies.   M a r s u p i a l s

14   In psychology, extreme self-love.   N a r c i s s i s m

15   Perennial plant of primrose family.   O . . . .

16   Figure of speech e.g. 'the child is father of the man'.   P . . . . . .

17   To interrogate.   Q . . .

18   A fried ball of minced food.   R . . . . . .

19   Desert rattlesnake of south west USA.   S . . . .

20   Large food-fish of the mackerel family.   T r o u t

21   Metallic element derived from pitchblende.   U r a n i u m

22   British architect; designed Blenheim Palace and Castle Howard.   V a n b r u g h

23   Peninsula in NW England between Dee and Mersey estuaries.   W i r r a l

24   The negative feminine and dark principle of Chinese philosophy and religion.   Y . .

FIFTY-FOUR

1   Robot with apparently human form.   A n d r o i d

67

2	Anti-tank rocket gun.	B *azouka*
3	Snake-like.	C . . . .
4	Large sofa.	D . . . .
5	Of great beauty or delicacy.	E . . . .
6	Depression on top of brick.	F *ill.*
7	Gypsy name for non-gypsy.	G . . . . .
8	Korean nymphs of paradise.	H *ouris*
9	Irritable, hot tempered.	I . . . .
10	Combat between two knights on horseback.	J *oust*
11	Tending to steal.	K . . . .
12	Jewellers' small magnifying glass.	L . . . .
13	Which American president was assassinated in 1901?	M . . . .
14	Juke-box.	N . . . .
15	Plane figure with eight sides.	O *ctagon*
16	Pastry cook's shop.	P *atisserie*
17	Recurring every third day.	Q . . . . . .
18	Artificial leather used in upholstery.	R . . . . .
19	Servile flatterer.	S *ycophant*
20	Evening drum or bugle signal.	T . . . . .
21	Large thin bone of the forearm.	U . . .
22	Case of puff pastry filled with meat.	V *ol-au-vent*
23	Nervous feeling.	W . . . . . .
24	Monetary unit of China.	Y . . .

FIFTY-FIVE

1 Plant classified as same genus as rhododendron.
A . . . . .

2 Who wrote 'Auld Lang Syne'?
B *Burns*

3 What land bird has the largest wing span?
C *ondor*

4 Despot ruler of Haiti from 1957-71.
D *uvalier*

5 Large lake in NE South Australia, much of which is perennially dry.
E . . .

6 Roman goddess of flowers.
F *lora*

7 German writer whose greatest work was the dramatic poem *Faust*.
G *oethe*

8 What is the profession of a trichologist?
H . . . .

9 What word connects Hebrides, Mongolia and temple?
I *nner*

10 Method of weaponless self-defence.
J . . . .

11 An electric motor-horn.
K . . . . .

12 Sexual desire.
L *ibido*

13 What would you find in Berwick Street, Leather Lane and Lower Marsh in London?
M *useums*

14 What was discovered by Galle in 1846?
N . . . . . .

15 Public official appointed to hear citizens' complaints.
O . . . .

16 A figure in old Italian comedy and French pantomime.
P . . . . . .

17 Capital of Equador.
Q *uito*

18 A platform for public speaking. R o s t r u m

19 Strait between S E Norway and N W Denmark. S Kagerrak

20 The 300th anniversary. T ercentenary

21 East German Head of State 1960–71. U . . . .

22 A sensation of dizziness. V ertigo

23 Young of herrings and sprats and a popular food-fish. W . . . .

24 A name in Italy for gypsies. Z . . . . . .

FIFTY-SIX

1 Liqueur of eggs, sugar and brandy. A dvocaat

2 Hard ring-shaped bread roll. B . . . .

3 Short witty verse. C . . . .

4 Ancient Roman silver coin. D enarius

5 Shameless insolence. E . . . .

6 Liveried servant. F . . . . . .

7 One of the three sisters whose look turned one to stone. G orgon

8 Clumsy awkward youth. H . . . .

9 The peninsula now comprising Spain and Portugal. I berian

10 Act nervously. J . . . . .

11 Eskimo one-man canoe. K ayak

12 Tincture of opium. L audanum

13 Pungent, smarting. M . . . . . .

14 Mother-of-pearl. N . . . .

15 Keep secret. O . . . . .

70

16 Pale especially from sickness. P . . . . .

17 A square or cube-like object. Q . . . .

18 Slovenly, coarsely outspoken. R . . . . . .

19 Drinking vessel. S . . . .

20 Sycophant. T *oady*

21 Edible offal of deer. U . . . . .

22 Needless accumulation of words. V *erbiage*

23 Indian civil servant. W *allah*

24 Italian sweet of eggs, sugar and wine. Z . . . .

FIFTY-SEVEN

1 Fear of heights. A *crophobia*

2 Who succeeded Ramsey Macdonald as Prime Minister in 1935? B *aldwin*

3 Who is called the 'father of English poetry'? C *haucer*

4 Who lived at 48 Doughty Street, London WC1? D *ickens*

5 Christian feast celebrated on 6 January. E *piphany*

6 American author whose works include *The Great Gatsby* (1925). F *itzgereld*

7 Root-like stem of the tropical plant, *Zingiber officinale*. G *inger*

8 Austrian composer of *The Creation*. H *aydn*

9 Bird of the stork family. I *bis*

10 World motor racing champion in 1980.   J . . . .

11 Loose robe with wide sleeves.   K . . . . .

12 Who sang *Roamin' in the Gloamin'*?   L . . . . .

13 Figure of speech e.g. 'she was pure gold'.   M *etaphor*

14 The study of coins and medals.   N . . . .

15 What word links the ruling family of the Netherlands, a town in France and a South African river?   O *range*

16 Study of system of language sounds.   P *honetics*

17 Alkaline powder obtained by strongly heating chalk.   Q . . . .

18 An ill-clad dirty person.   R *agamuffin*

19 Antirrhinum.   S . . . .

20 Phoenician town sacked by Alexander the Great.   T *yre*

21 Reddish-brown wild sheep of N. India and Tibet.   U . . . .

22 A room adjoining a church.   V *estry*

23 Woodland game-bird.   W . . . .

24 A corpse reanimated by sorcery.   Z *ombie*

FIFTY-EIGHT

1 Disease of sheep and cattle.   A *nthrax*

2 Divide into two branches.   B . . . .

3 Puma. — C . . . .

4 Light brown raw cane sugar. — D *emerera*

5 Shoulder piece on uniform. — E *paulette*

6 Of fever. — F . . . .

7 Highland cap with pointed front. — G . . . .

8 Inflammation of the liver. — H *epatitis*

9 Allusive remark usually depreciatory. — I . . . .

10 Shameless woman. — J *ezebel*

11 Fine cotton material used for stuffing. — K . . . .

12 Member of English artisans who rioted. — L . . . . . .

13 Indefinitely great number. — M . . . . .

14 City in south-east France. — N *ice*

15 Tapered monolithic shaft. — O *belisk*

16 Abode of all demons. — P . . . .

17 Coats marshalled on a shield. — Q *uarterings*

18 Scale for denoting strength of earthquakes. — R *ichter*

19 Young salmon. — S . . . . .

20 Light meal. — T . . . . .

21 Rain-gauge. — U . . . .

22 Duct shaped. — V *olcanis*

23 African gnu. — W *ildebeast*

24 Woody tissue. — X . . . .

FIFTY-NINE

1   A word, e.g. laser, which is formed from the initial letters of other words.

A . . . . . .

2   What battle claimed the life of Richard III?

B osworth

3   What are Enck's, Biela's and Donati's?

C . . . . .

4   River which flows from the Black Forest to the Black Sea.

D anube

5   A puzzling person or thing.

E . . . . .

6   Small instrument of flute family.

F ife

7   What became British during the War of the Spanish Succession in 1704?

G ibraltar

8   Anglo-Saxon chieftain and brother of Hengist.

H orsa

9   Light given out by a body when raised to intense white heat.

I . . . .

10   English physician; discoverer of vaccination.

J . . . . .

11   Type of court operated by an improperly constituted body.

K . . . .

12   The seed of the flax plant which yields oil when crushed.

L inseed

13   Last of the Aztec rulers of Mexico.

M ontezuma

14   What name connects an island in the West Indies and a mountain.

N evis

15 Allium cepa, biennial plant of the lily family, native to SW Asia.

O . . . .

16 Who first reached the North Pole?

P . . . .

17 International phonetic code name for 'q'.

Q . . . . .

18 First Director-General of the BBC.

R *eith*

19 Official language of Sri Lanka.

S *inhalese*

20 Former name of the Near-East country now known as Jordan.

T *ransjordan*

21 To wail in lamentation.

U *lulate*

22 To clear from blame.

V *indicate*

23 Marine mammal related to the seal.

W *alrus*

24 The positive masculine and light principle of Chinese philosophy and religion.

Y *ang*

SIXTY

1 Medium-dry sherry of a matured type.

A *montillado*

2 Gratuity or tip.

B . . . .

3 Neapolitan ice-cream with fruit and nuts.

C . . . . . .

4 Cocktail of rum and lime juice.

D . . . . . .

5 Bringing about an easy and gentle death.

E *uthanasia*

6   Device for enabling aircraft to
land in fog.   F . . .

7   Street urchin.   G a m i a

8   Break in a series.   H . . . . .

9   Breaker of images.   I c o n o c l a s t

10   Doleful prophet.   J e r e m i a h

11   Australian marsupial.   K o a l a

12   Young hare.   L . . . . .

13   Low floor between two
others.   M e z z a n i n e

14   Wrestling hold.   N . . . . .

15   Leopard-like feline.   O . . . . .

16   Thick-skinned mammal.   P a c h i d e r m

17   Set of 4 aces, 4 kings, 4
queens, or 4 jacks in one hand at
piquet.   Q . . . .

18   Full of chinks or fissures.   R a g g e d

19   Cutting, division.   S . . . . . .

20   Brownish yellow.   T a w n y

21   Duct from bladder.   U r e t h a

22   Person eating no animal
products.   V e g a n

23   Piece of open uncultivated
land.   W . . .

24   Sword shaped.   X . . . . . .

SIXTY-ONE
_____

1   City in Georgia, burned by
Sherman during American Civil
War.   A t l a n t a

2   Chief ore of aluminium.   B . . . . . .

76

3 What alkaloid is found in the leaves of the coco plant of South America?

C cocaine

4 Title of eldest son of kings of France.

D dauphin

5 To throw light on.

E enlighten

6 Rubber plant.

F . . . .

7 Who said 'in two words: impossible'?

G . . . . . .

8 Greek physician known as the father of medicine.

H ippocrates

9 Freedom from possibility of error.

I nfallibility

10 Leader of the Israelites after the death of Moses.

J oshua

11 Paraffin-oil obtained by distillation of petroleum.

K . . . .

12 Process of taking an action to court for settlement.

L itigation

13 Where would you find the tomb of the prophet Mohammed?

M . . . . .

14 Greek goddess of retribution.

N . . . . . .

15 Going out of use.

O bselescent

16 Triangular structure crowning the front of a building.

P . . . .

17 Standard typewriter keyboard layout.

Q . . . . .

18 Ruling house of Russia from 1613–1917.

R omanov

19 Old literary language of India.

S anscrit

20 What are catalpa, koelreuteria and styrax?

T . . . .

21 Mountain range west of central USSR.

U rals

22 A wine-seller.   V i n t n e r

23 Twisted thread or yarn spun out of long combed wool.   W . . . . . .

24 A small fishing boat.   Y . . .

SIXTY-TWO

1 Waxlike odiferous substance found floating in tropical seas.   A . . . .

2 Red or white Burgundy wine.   B . . . .

3 Steep gully.   C . . . . . .

4 The study of trees.   D . . . .

5 Burden.   E . . . .

6 Small flute blown at the end like a recorder.   F . . . .

7 Light filmy substance like the web of a spider.   G . . . .

8 Witty servant in Italian comedy.   H . . . .

9 Narrow piece of land connecting two larger bodies of land.   I s t h m u s

10 Pert fellow or tame monkey.   J . . . .

11 Sweet liqueur.   K . . . . .

12 Thin plate.   L . . . . . .

13 Woman's loose brightly-coloured dress.   M . .-. . .

14 Hot sweetened wine and water.   N . . . .

15 Dark kind of China tea.   O . . . . .

16 Words that read the same backwards or forwards.   P . . . .

17 Ancient chariot with four horses abreast.   Q . . . .

18	Small monkey.	R . . . . .
19	Light open carriage for one.	S . . . .
20	Conical tent of American Indians.	T *epee*
21	20th Greek letter.	U . . . . . .
22	Tending to become green.	V . . . .
23	Seaweed cast up and used for manure.	W . . . .
24	The green woodpecker.	Y . . . . .

SIXTY-THREE

1	Stage-name of Frederick Austerlitz.	A . . . . . .
2	Inland South American state.	B . . . . .
3	What is the game of draughts known as in North America?	C . . . .
4	French composer whose works include *Clair de Lune*.	D . . . . . .
5	A writing-desk.	E . . . .
6	An apparently genuine but really illogical argument.	F *fallacy*
7	Place in Somerset said to have been visited by Joseph of Arimathea.	G *lastonbury*
8	Instrument for detecting under-water sounds.	H . . . .
9	Branch of biology concerned with study of fishes.	I . . . .
10	Throw goods overboard to save a vessel or the rest of the cargo.	J *ettison*
11	Castle which is scene of Shakespeare's *Hamlet*.	K . . . .

79

12 Breed of horse developed in Austria. L . . . .

13 Who is Jean Baptiste Poquelin, French dramatist, better known as. M o l i e r e

14 Favouritism shown to relations in bestowing office. N e p o t i s m

15 What were first seen on the streets of London in 1829? O . . . .

16 The first five books of the Bible. P e n t a t e u c h

17 The bitter extraction of the bark of the cinchona tree. Q . . . . .

18 What word links a family of birds with the uttering of angry taunts. R . . .

19 Amphibious lizard-like creature. S a l a m a n d e r

20 A cave dweller. T . . . .

21 Cathedral and university city of east Sweden. U p p s a l a

22 A skilful musician. V i r t u o s o

23 English aeronautical engineer who designed the bouncing bomb. W . . . . .

24 To cry mournfully. Y o w l

SIXTY-FOUR

1 The opposite of perigee. A . . . . .

2 Fine cloth made of wool. B . . . .

3 Of twilight. C . . . .

4 Game with two-headed top and string. D . . . . .

5 Honourably discharged from service. E . . . .

80

6 Ornamental work in silver or gold thread. F . . . . .

7 Colloquial name for New York City. G otham

8 Offspring of she-ass and stallion. H . . . .

9 The letter Z. I . . . . .

10 Playful. J . . . . .

11 Health resort casino. K . . . . . .

12 Young street urchin. L . . . . .

13 Having appearance of metal. M . . . .

14 Water nymph. N aiad

15 Mounted guns. O . . . .

16 Illicit lover. P aramour

17 Person between 40 and 49 years old. Q uadragenarian

18 Of river banks. R . . . .

19 Track or scent of animals. S . . . .

20 Small mountain lake. T . . .

21 A poisonous tree from Java. U . . .

22 Odin's handmaidens, twelve in number. V alkyrie

23 Small curlew. W . . . .

24 Part of a house in which women of high caste are secluded in Iran. Z . . . . .

SIXTY-FIVE

1 Truce before signing a peace treaty. A rmistice

2 Writer of *Prester John*. B uchan

81

3 Which native of Poland, who died in 1543, is known as the founder of modern astronomy?

C *Copernicus*

4 Where would you find Dover and Wilmington?

D *Delaware*

5 An American card game.

E . . . . .

6 A water tap.

F *Faucet*

7 French island in the West Indies.

G *Guadaloupe*

8 British battleship sunk by the Bismark in 1941.

H . . .

9 To attack by words or arguments.

I . . . . .

10 Carnivorous animal closely related to the wolf.

J *Jackal*

11 The Buddhist conception of the quality of a person's actions.

K *Karma*

12 Name of the bell at Lloyds of London which announces shipping losses.

L . . . . .

13 Italian composer of *Cavalleria Rusticana*.

M *Massenet*

14 A bunch of fragrant flowers.

N . . . . . .

15 Compounds of any element with oxygen.

O . . . . .

16 What name connects a town in Scotland with a vociferous politician?

P *Paisley*

17 Norwegian who collaborated with Germany in 1940, whose name became synonymous with traitor.

Q . . . .

18 American writer whose works include *Guys and Dolls*.

R *Runyon*

82

19 What game is the indoor derivation of baseball? S *oftball*

20 A machine on which cloth is stretched by hooks. T . . . . .

21 In Greek myth, personification of heavens. U *ranus*

22 What in America is the Green Mountain State? V *ermont*

23 American exponent of pop art. W *arhol*

24 Irish poet and dramatist and winner of 1923 Nobel Prize for Literature. Y *eats*

SIXTY-SIX

1 Gully. A . . . . .

2 Deadly nightshade. B . . . .

3 Lava flow. C . . . . .

4 Triangular. D . . . . . .

5 Imitation. E . . . . . .

6 Hoop of whalebone worn under dress. F . . . .

7 Structure from which view may be obtained. G . . . . .

8 Shaggy. H . . . . .

9 Bone in the pelvis. I . . . .

10 Small Spanish horse. J . . . . .

11 Difficult to deal with. K . . . . .

12 Poor and diseased person. L . . . .

13 Small caster for sprinkling sugar. M . . . .

14 Blackness. N *igritude*

15	Wild ass.	O . . . . .
16	Complete suit of armour.	P . . . . . .
17	Using four transmission channels.	Q . . . .
18	One who relapses into crime.	R . . . .
19	Family tree.	S . . . . .
20	Chinese seven piece puzzle.	T . . . . . .
21	Sting like a nettle.	U . . . .
22	Thin coating of ice.	V . . . . . .
23	Narrow street.	W . . .
24	Administrative district in India.	Z . . . .

SIXTY-SEVEN

1	A bee-keeper.	A . . . .
2	Plants of the cabbage family including broccoli and kale.	B . . . .
3	What were Richard Tarleton, Robert Armin and Joseph Grimaldi?	C . . . . .
4	Scottish chemist who developed the vacuum flask.	D . . . .
5	Twin brother of Jacob.	E Sau
6	Capital of Madeira Islands.	F . . . . . .
7	Dance starting on the third beat of a four-pulse measure.	G avotte
8	The art of making machines to measure time.	H . . . .
9	The power of authority of an emperor.	Imperialism
10	Either of two large veins in the neck.	Jugular

84

11 Artificial lake on river Zambezi formed by the construction of a dam in 1959.

K _Kaunda_

12 Bushy-tailed mammal related to monkeys.

L _Lemur_

13 Who did Doyle describe as the Napoleon of crime in *The Final Problem*?

M _Moriarty_

14 The Old Bailey stands on the site of which prison?

N . . . . . .

15 Members of protestant society formed in Ulster in 1795.

O _Orangemen_

16 Roman general who with Caesar and Crassus formed first Triumverate.

P _ompey_

17 Once in four years.

Q . . . .

18 What was the sport of the late Henri Toivonen?

R . . . . . .

19 What shape is a volute?

S _quare_

20 Act of twisting or turning a body.

T . . . . . .

21 Official language of Pakistan.

U _rdu_

22 Pertaining to glass.

V . . . . . .

23 Common food-fish of the cod family.

W . . . . . .

24 Suburb of New York.

Y _onkers_

SIXTY-EIGHT

1 In the open air.

A . . . .

2 Wild Norse warrior fighting with mad frenzy.

B _erserker_ .

3 Club shaped.

C . . . . . .

85

4   Chief magistrate of Venice.   D o g e

5   Cluster of electric lamps.   E . . . .

6   Egyptian labourer.   F . . . .

7   Automaton.   G . . . .

8   Hairy.   H . . . .

9   Final stage of an insect after metamorphosis.   I . . . .

10   Opaque variety of quartz.   J . . . . .

11   Fancy dish in cooking.   K . . . .

12   Indian sailor.   L . . . . .

13   Monkish.   M . . . . .

14   Knotty.   N . . . . .

15   Place where Greeks consulted their deity.   O r a c l e

16   Open plane curve, section of a cone.   P a r a b o l a

17   Short handled riding stick.   Q . . . .

18   Of the nose.   R . . . . .

19   Shaped like an arrow head.   S h a r p e n e d

20   Sheep in its second year.   T . .

21   Pitcher shaped.   U . . . .

22   Of a veil.   V . . . .

23   Wind pipe.   W . . . . . .

24   Hot dusty wind of northern Argentine.   Z . . . .

SIXTY-NINE

1   Scientific study of man.   A n t h r o p o l o g y

2   Who is Gautama Siddhartha, born India 500 BC, better known as?   B u d d h a

3   Who was known in theatrical circles as 'The Master'?   C . . . . .

4 French fashion designer. D *ior*

5 Composer of *The Dream of Gerontius.* E *lgar*

6 Japan's highest mountain. F *ujiyama*

7 The name of six Swedish kings from 1496–1973. G *ustavus*

8 Apparatus for measuring the density of a liquid. H . . . .

9 Islands of western Greece including Corfu and Levkas. I *onian*

10 Naval battle, fought on 31 May 1916 between Britain and Germany. J *utland*

11 Capital of Zaire. K *inshasa*

12 What consists of a fungus and an alga plant living together? L . . . . .

13 Winner of cycling's Tour de France five times from 1969–1974. M . . . . .

14 Term applied by astronomers to an exploding star. N *ova*

15 Musical interval, or scale, of eight notes. O *ctave*

16 Who described Nell Gwynne as 'pretty witty Nell'? P *epys*

17 Small tree, native to Asia, which bears pear-shaped fruit used in preserves. Q *uince*

18 Currency unit of Saudi Arabia. R *iyal*

19 Branch of grammar dealing with sentences and their construction. S *yntax*

20 Large edible species of flat-fish. T *urbot*

21   Province of central Netherlands.   U _Utrecht_

22   What name connects a musical instrument and a plant?   V _iola_

23   What are La Guayra and Kaieteur?   W . . . .

24   Greek philosopher famous for a series of paradoxes.   Z _eno_

SEVENTY

1   Member of the class containing spiders.   A _rachnids_

2   Two headed.   B . . . .

3   Sperm whale.   C . . . .

4   Of the day.   D . . . . . .

5   Upper or outer curve of an arch.   E . . . . . .

6   Of a river.   F . . . . . .

7   Enigmatic smiler.   G . . . .

8   Strong linen cloth.   H . . . .

9   Fish-like.   I . . . .

10   Turkish sultan's guard.   J _anissary_.

11   Commotion.   K . . . .

12   Mixture of cresols and soft soap.   L _athe_

13   Monkey.   M . . . . . .

14   Small round piece of meat.   N _oisette_

15   Concerned with smelling.   O . . . .

16   Universal remedy.   P _anacea_

17   Result given by dividing one quantity by another.   Q _uotient_

18   Root-like.   R . . . . . .

19 Spider monkey.   S . . . . . .

20 Clay oven.   T *andoor*

21 Dweller in the city.   U *rbanite*

22 Stone shaped by wind-blown
sand.   V . . . .

23 Maoiri house.   W . . . .

24 Fermentation.   Z . . . . . .

SEVENTY-ONE

1 Monk of Iona who became
Bishop of Lindisfarne.   A *iden*

2 Ancient name for
Constantinople (Istanbul).   B *yzantium*

3 What horse race is named
after a Russian prince?   C . . . .

4 Large sand bank off
Northumberland in North Sea.   D . . . . .

5 Writer of thirteen books of
theorems and problems collectively
named *The Elements*.   E *uclid*

6 Market and meeting place of
Roman towns.   F *orum*

7 Star of the film *Kind Hearts and
Coronets*.   G *uinness*

8 Small organ in which the
sound is produced by forcing air
through reeds.   H *armonium*

9 Of low birth.   I *gnoble*

10 Old motor-car or aeroplane.   J . . . . .

11 African tribal group who led
by Jomo Kenyatta fought the
British in the Mau Mau uprising.   K . . . . .

12 Ball game between two teams of twelve players.

L a c r o s s e

13 Document signed by ship's captain detailing its cargo.

M . . . .

14 International phonetic code name for 'n'.

N . . . .

15 Form of speech e.g. 'murmuring of innumerable bees'.

O n o m a t o p o e i a

16 Pacific islands which include Tonga and Samoa.

P o l y n e s i a

17 A boggy place.

Q u a g

18 What stone discovered in 1799 was the key to deciphering Egyptian hieroglyphics?

R o s s e t t a

19 What are abutilon, callicarpa and clethra?

S . . . . .

20 Site near Marble Arch in London where executions took place up to 1784.

T y b u r n

21 Side-splittingly funny.

U p r o a r i o u s

22 Star whose brightness varies, either periodically or irregularly.

V . . . .

23 English aeronautic engineer who patented designs for turbo-jet engine.

W . . . . . .

24 Both a country and a river in central Africa.

Z a i r e

SEVENTY-TWO

1 Lady's maid.

A . . . . . .

2 Enormous creature.

B . . . .

3 A shelter at a beach.

C . . . . .

4 Inhabitant or occupant.

D . . . . . .

5 Species of wheat.   E . . . . . .

6 Giddy flirtatious young
woman.   F . . . . .

7 Tree with fan-shaped leaves
and yellow flowers.   G . . . . .

8 Meat to make minced loaf.   H . . . . .

9 Jaundice.   I . . . . . .

10 Slatted shutter or blind.   J . . . .

11 Game like basketball.   K . . . .

12 Lute player.   L . . . .

13 Low, marshy, unhealthy
country by the seashore.   M . . . . . .

14 Sea nymph.   N . . . . .

15 Native of the Orkney Islands.   O . . . .

16 African tool like a machette.   P . . . .

17 Padded bedcover.   Q *uilt*

18 Vitamin B2.   R . . . .

19 Groove or furrow.   S . . . . .

20 Bull-like.   T . . . . . .

21 Growing in wet and swampy
places.   U . . . .

22 Of worms.   V . . . . . .

23 Decorated shells used by
North American Indians as
money.   W . . . . .

24 Sword without guard used in
Muslim countries.   Y . . . .

SEVENTY-THREE

1 Headmaster of Rugby School
who reformed English public
school system.   A *rnold*

91

2   Author of *Pilgrim's Progress*.   B u n y a n

3   Who was portrayed by James Cagney in the film *Yankee Doodle Dandy*?   C o h a n

4   Cavalry soldier trained to fight on foot.   D r a g o o n

5   Who sculptured 'Behold The Man'?   E p s t e i n

6   Any of *lampyridae* family of luminescent beetles.   F i r e f l y

7   Long-billed diving bird.   G . . . .

8   Pioneer of jazz, who composed the Memphis Blues in 1910.   H . . . .

9   Line on a map connecting points of equal temperature.   I . . . .

10   Religious beliefs and observances of the Jews.   J u d a i s m

11   English poet who wrote *Ode to a Nightingale*.   K e a t s

12   Who called Schubert the 'most poetic of musicians'?   L i s z t

13   Container serving twelve glasses of champagne.   M . . . . .

14   In the Bible, who was the mother-in-law of Ruth?   N a o m i

15   What type of column is Cleopatra's Needle?   O b e l i s k

16   Stately dance of Poland, usually in three-four time.   P o l o n a i s e

17   Mental tranquillity.   Q . . . .

18   Stream in central Italy crossed by Julius Caesar in 49 BC.   R u b i c o n

19   Three types of sword are used in fencing, foil and epeé are two, which is the third?   S a b r e

20   River which joins with the Ouse to form the Humber.   T r e n t

21   French painter who specialized in Parisian street scenes.   U . . . . . .

22   A wandering of the thoughts.   V . . . . .

23   A wooden-panelled lining applied to the walls of a room.   W . . . .

24   Book of Old Testament.   Z e c h a r i a h

SEVENTY-FOUR

1   Magistrate in Spanish town.   A . . . . .

2   Potted small tree.   B o n s a i

3   Giraffe.   C . . . .

4   Of the back.   D . . . . .

5   Lean-bodied person.   E . . . .

6   Performed very loudly.   F . . . .

7   Of the tongue.   G . . . .

8   Manikin.   H o m u n c u l u s

9   Leader of prayer in a Mosque.   I m a m

10   Australian mahogany gum tree.   J . . . . .

11   Body of female insect.   K . . . . .

12   Shaped like a lance.   L . . . .

13   Mixture of wine, oil, vinegar, herbs and spices.   M . . . .

14   Of the nape of the neck.   N . . . . .

15   Mountain nymph.   O . . . .

16   Gingerbread made with oatmeal and treacle.   P . . . . .

17   Fourfold.   Q . . . .

18 West Indian style of music with strong beat. R . . . . .

19 Piece of bony armour in crocodile. S . . . . .

20 Composed of three parts. T . . . . . .

21 European cavalry man armed with lance. U . . . .

22 Chicken pox. V . . . .

23 Reddish-brown and grey North American marmot. W . . . .

24 Bony arch of cheek. Z . . . . .

SEVENTY-FIVE

1 First Roman emperor, full name Gaius Julius Caesar Octavianus. A ugustus

2 Three-masted sailing-ship. B . . . . .

3 Pen name of Charles Lutwidge Dodgson. C arroll

4 American singer-composer born Robert Zimmerman. D ylan

5 Meaning of the Latin word *ubique*. E . . . .

6 Deciduous shrub whose yellow flowers appear before its leaves. F orsythia

7 What style of architecture is the Notre Dame in Paris? G othic

8 19th-Century German physicist who has a unit of frequency named after him. H ertz

9 Group of five North American Indian tribes. I . . . .

10 What calendar was observed in England until 1752? J ulian

11 Where is Lake Magadi? Kenya

12 Small Baltic state incorporated into the USSR in 1940. Lithuania

13 Dance with three slowish beats to the bar. Minuet

14 What horse won the 2000 Guineas, Derby and St Leger in 1970? N . . . .

15 Gilt or bronzed metallic ware. O . . . . .

16 Member of Jewish sect at time of Christ. Pharasee

17 A Roman magistrate. Q . . . .

18 Freshwater fish of carp family. R . . . .

19 In ice-skating, what is the name of a jump off the back inside edge of one foot? S . . . . . .

20 Capital of Albania. Tirana

21 To take possession of by force without the right to do so. Usurp

22 In Norse myth, banqueting hall in Asgard, home of the gods. Valhalla

23 20th-century composer whose works include *The Threepenny Opera*. Weill

24 West Belgium town which was the scene of three battles in World War I. Ypres

SEVENTY-SIX

1 Of tooth socket. A . . . .

2   Shanty town built of oil
drums.   B . . . .

3   Crab like.   C . . . .

4   Wraith of living person.   D . . . . . \ . . .

5   Growing abnormally.   E . . . .

6   Creator of James Bond.   F *leming*

7   Machine gun with clustered
barrels.   G . . . . . .

8   Nymph living and dying with
a tree.   H . . . .

9   Engraving or carving on a
sunken ground.   I . . . .)

10   Reckless driver.   J . . . '

11   Knot in wood.   K . . .

12   Thrash or beat.   L . . . .

13   Elephant driver.   M . . . . .

14   Execution by drowning.   N . . . . .

15   Solver of riddles.   O . . . . .

16   Bird similar to a sparrow.   P . . . .

17   Occurring once in every five
years.   Q . . . .

18   Bending downwards.   R . . . .

19   Quality perceptible by taste.   S . . . .

20   Small draught of brandy.   T . . .

21   Whisky.   U . . . .

22   Of violet colour.   V . . . .

23   Anti-clockwise.   W . . . .

24   Principal protein of maize.   Z . . .

SEVENTY-SEVEN

1   Courthouse where Lee
surrendered to Grant in 1865.   A *ppomattox*

2   Gold and silver not yet made into coins.

B ullion

3   Mountainous island off south coast of France.

C orsica

4   A solid figure with ten faces.

D ecahedron

5   Eruptive disease of the skin.

E . . . . .

6   American economist and influential advocate of monetarist policies.

F . . . . . .

7   Small burrowing rodent of North America.

G opher

8   German president who appointed Adolf Hitler Chancellor in 1933.

H indenburg

9   In philosophy the theory that nothing outside ideas has any reality.

I dealism

10   Supporters in the 18th century of the exiled Stuarts.

J acobites

11   The science of motion without reference to force.

K inematics

12   British architect and designer of the Cenotaph in Whitehall, London.

L . . . . . .

13   Capital of Nicaragua.

M anagua

14   A sorcerer.

N ecromancer

15   Government by a small exclusive class.

O . . . .

16   One of Alexander the Great's generals who became king of Egypt.

P tolemy

17   A stanza of four lines usually rhyming alternately.

Q . . . .

18   In which mountain range is Mount Elias?

R ockies

19 Stretch of water you would cross when travelling from Southsea to Ryde.

S . . . . .

20 Famous town in Mali dating back to 11th century, centre of caravan trade routes.

T *imbuktu*

21 Instrument or vessel used in common life.

U . . . . . .

22 Italian navigator whose first name, Amerigo, led to name America.

V . . . .

23 Where would you find Madison and Milwaukee?

W *isconsin*

24 Town of USSR which was the scene in 1945 of a meeting between Churchill, Roosevelt and Stalin.

Y *alta*

SEVENTY-EIGHT

1 Sea with many islands.

A *rchipelago*

2 Triangular bodied guitar-like musical instrument.

B . . . .

3 A coil or mass of hair.

C . . . . . .

4 Small country villa in Russia.

D *acha*

5 Forcible extraction.

E . . . .

6 Curved like a sickle.

F . . . .

7 Cylinder of wicker or woven metal bands.

G . . . . .

8 Remarkable person.

H . . . .

9 Overlap like tiles on a roof.

I . . . .

10 Tropical American tree.

J *acaranda*

11 One of the Turkish pastoral people.

K *urd*

12 Yielding milk.   L . . . .

13 Shore grass that binds sand.   M . . . . .

14 Bright orange-red colour.   N . . . . . .

15 Sorcery practised by Negroes.   O . . . .

16 Of the palm of the hand.   P . . . . .

17 Discharge from a debt.   Q . . . .

18 Meat in small pieces stewed with vegetables.   R . . . . .

19 Who wrote *Gulliver's Travels*.   S *wift*

20 Newspaper printed on half-sized sheets.   T *abloid*

21 Which fabulous animal appears in the royal arms of England?   U *nicorn*

22 What is the green poisonous deposit formed on copper?   V . . . .

23 What is a male witch called?   W *arlock*

24 In Greek mythology, the chief of the gods.   Z *eus*

SEVENTY-NINE

1 What type of vegetable is 'green globe'?   A . . . .

2 Who did Joe Louis K O in round 8 to win his first world heavyweight championship?   B . . . .

3 Creator of *Don Quixote*.   C *ervantes*

4 A cowardly fellow.   D . . . . . .

5 American aviator who was first woman to fly Atlantic solo (1932).   E . . . . . .

6   Where would you find Tallahassee and Jacksonville?   F l o r i d a

7   Heights which form a strategic mountain range of S W Syria.   G o l a n

8   Any plant which turns to face the sun.   H e l i o t r o p e

9   Peculiarity of temperament or mental constitution.   I . . . .

10   Mountain of west central Switzerland in Bernese Oberland.   J u n g f r a u

11   Cabbage with a turnip-shaped stem.   K . . . .

12   Protestant bishop and martyr during the Reformation.   L a t i m e r

13   Capital of Burma from 1857–85 only.   M a n d e l a y

14   To wink.   N . . . . . .

15   Instrument which shows the distance travelled by a wheel.   O . . . .

16   Greek name for Neptune, god of the sea.   P o s e i d o n

17   City in the Philippines.   Q u e z o n

18   What are Elizabeth of Glamis, Fred Loads and Yellow Doll?   R . . . .

19   Musical based on an Edna Ferber novel.   S . . . .

20   Roman emperor who succeeded Augustus in A D 14.   T i b e r i u s

21   Not prudent or discreet.   U . . . .

22   Genus of American orchid whose pod-like capsule yields flavouring extract.   V . . . . . .

23   Writer of *The Four Just Men*.   W . . . . . .

24   Rare metallic element with the symbol Yb.

Y . . . .

EIGHTY

1   Legendary heroes who sailed with Jason.

A rgonauts

2   Caning on the soles of the foot.

B . . . .

3   Red-legged crow.

C . . . . .

4   Plane figure with ten sides.

D ecagon

5   Group of bees.

E . . .

6   Species of thrush.

F . . . .

7   Mollusc, snail, limpet, etc.

G . . . .

8   Pellets of frozen rain.

H ail

9   In which state is Chicago?

I llinois

10   Pianist and composer of ragtime music.

J oplin

11   Carnivorous arboreal animal.

K . . . .

12   S American mammal related to the camel.

L lama

13   Noxious emanation.

M . . . . .

14   Poisonous alkaloid substance in tobacco.

N icotine

15   King of the fairies in *A Midsummer Night's Dream*.

O beron

16   Web-footed bird.

P . . . .

17   Borough of New York City.

Q ueens

18   Real estate agent.

R . . . . . .

19   Group of islands lie N E of the Orkneys.

S hetland

20   Small drum.

T abor

21 What is hypogeal? U . . . .

22 Which S American bat sucks the blood of sleeping animals? V ampire

23 Thick-lipped brightly-coloured fish. W . . . . .

24 American university of New Haven, Connecticut (Founded 1701). Y ale

EIGHTY-ONE

1 A description of one thing under the image of another. A . . . .

2 Aviator who held the air speed record in 1909. B . . . . . .

3 Green colouring matter present in plants. C horophyll

4 What is the profession of an odontologist? D entist

5 Any of *dermaptera* order of insects. E . . . . .

6 City of S Western Australia. F . . . .

7 American band leader and clarinettist. G . . . . . .

8 Apparatus for measuring the moisture of the atmosphere. H . . . .

9 A metrical foot of two syllables. I ambus

10 The SI unit of work, energy, heat. J oule

11 Desert of Botswana and NE South Africa. K alahari

12 Small Baltic state incorporated into the USSR in 1940. L atvia

13 Family of very small monkeys. M . . . .

14 Ghanaian political leader overthrown by army coup in 1966. N . . . . . .

15 What name connects weight and leopard? O unce

16 What was Englishman Nicholas Breakspeare from 1154–9? P ope

17 Extinct South African zebra. Q . . . . .

18 Which American mountain contains the carved faces of four American presidents? R ushmore

19 Which English poet was drowned in Italy? S helley

20 Who wrote *Barchester Towers*? T hackery

21 Long and loose kind of overcoat. U . . . . .

22 Latin version of the Bible made by St Jerome AD 346–420. V ulgata

23 Island group in West Indies which includes Dominica and St Vincent. W indward

24 Fear or hatred of strangers. X enophobia

EIGHTY-TWO

1 Chinese nursemaid. A . . .
2 Large destructive rat. B . . . .
3 Medley of sounds. C . . . .
4 Small coffee cup. D . . . .

5	Small one-horse vehicle.	E . . .
6	Type of flamenco dance.	F . . . . .
7	Organ stop with string tone.	G . . . .
8	Crouch or squat.	H . . . . .
9	Fluid flowing like blood in the veins of a god.	I . . . .
10	African desert rodent.	J . . . . .
11	Group of teal.	K . . .
12	Of a lake.	L . . . .
13	Musk-flavoured grape.	M *Muscadine*
14	Yellow cotton cloth.	N . . . . . .
15	Back of the head.	O . . . . . .
16	Pompous official or pretender.	P . . . .
17	Equation where x is raised to a power or indices.	Q *uadratic*
18	Group of penguins.	R . . . . . .
19	Which is the brightest star in the sky?	S . . . . .
20	Outer garment worn by Romans.	T *oga*
21	Affording shade.	U . . . .
22	Nest of wasps.	V . . . .
23	What is the House of Hanover called today?	W *indsor*
24	US theatrical producer of lavish follies and revues in 1920s.	Z *iegfeldt*

EIGHTY-THREE

| 1 | Venue of the 1920 Olympic Games. | A . . . . . . |

104

2 Group of plants with long tapering roots rich in sugar. B . . .

3 Group of animals which include crabs, crayfish and water-fleas. C rustaceans

4 The red-backed sandpiper. D . . . . .

5 Russian film director who pioneered cinematic techniques. E isenstein

6 American president 1850–3. F . . . .

7 Nazi propaganda minister (1933–45). G oebbels

8 Astronomer Royal from 1720, who studied the motion of comets. H alley

9 Who was the first English actor to be knighted (May 1895)? I rving

10 Container serving twenty-four glasses of champagne. J . . . .

11 Chief seaport of Pakistan. K arachi

12 Which capital city lies near the mouth of the River Tagus? L isbon

13 Famous family of bankers in Florence. M edici

14 Fourth Book of Pentateuch in Old Testament. N umbers

15 Secret rites observed in the worship of Bacchus. O ccult

16 Feather-shaped. P . . . .

17 Site in west Jordan of discovery in 1947 of the Dead Sea Scrolls. Q umran

18 Discoverer of X-rays. R . . . . . .

19 Figure of speech e.g. 'black as pitch'. S imile

20 English author whose works include *The Hobbit*.   T olkein

21 An anointing.   U . . . . . .

22 Cape which is most western point of Africa.   V erde

23 British politician who campaigned for abolition of slavery.   W ilberforce.

24 Scene of surrender, in 1781, of British forces at end of American Revolution.   Y orktown

EIGHTY-FOUR

1 Jumping movement in skating.   A . . .

2 Fabulous reptile hatched by serpent from a cock's egg.   B . . . .

3 Prison.   C . . . .

4 Right-handed person.   D . . . . . .

5 Centre ornament for dining table.   E . . . .

6 Dead leaf colour, brownish yellow.   F . . . . . .

7 Mixture of petrol and alcohol used as fuel.   G . . . . . .

8 Sunstroke.   H . . . .

9 Solid with twenty triangular faces.   I cosahedron

10 Which is the largest of the planets?   J upiter

11 Hot S E wind in Egypt.   K . . . . . .

12 Large estates.   L . . . .

13 Threatening.   M . . . .

14 Casserole of lamb with vegetables.   N . . . . . .

15 Having scent.   O *odorous*

16 Elevation of earth behind fortifications.   P . . . . . .

17 A figure on a post for tilting at.   Q . . . .

18 Infectious disease of ruminants.   R . . . .

19 Of the squirrel family.   S . . . . . .

20 Causing darkness.   T . . . .

21 Awkward.   U . . . . . .

22 Each of the wedge-shaped stones forming an arch.   V . . . .

23 Having large prominent eyes.   W . . . .

24 Carnivorous African quadruped allied to skunk and weasel.   Z . . . .

EIGHTY-FIVE
_____

1 British general who captured Jerusalem in 1917.   A *llenby*

2 What is pugilism?   B . . . . .

3 Wedge-shaped writing.   C *uneiform*

4 A little hollow, usually with trees.   D . . .

5 The study of man in relation to his working environment.   E . . . .

6 Small merchant vessel used in the Mediterranean.   F *elucca*

7 German who committed suicide after Nuremberg trials.   G *oering*

107

8 Who first appeared in *A Study in Scarlet*? H olmes

9 Alloy composed of 64 per cent iron, 36 per cent nickel. I . . . .

10 Better known name of spiky shrub, flowering quince. J . . . .

11 South African native village. K . . . .

12 River which runs through Dublin. L . . . . .

13 What would you find on Great Russell Street, Lambeth Road and Cromwell Road in London? M useums

14 Zimbabwean politician. N kome

15 System of healing by manipulation and massage. O . . . .

16 A lighthouse or beacon. P . . . . .

17 An ancient ship with five rows of oarsmen of each side. Q . . . .

18 British painter and first president of Royal Academy. R eynolds

19 What is meant by the musical term 'lagato'? S mooth

20 Birthplace of St Paul. T arsus

21 The dark cone projected by a planet on the side opposite to the sun. U mbra

22 Author of *Around the World in Eighty Days*. V erne

23 Piece of furniture with shelves to hold anything. W . . . . . .

24 Territory of N W Canada which dramatically increased in population during Klondike gold rush (1896). Y ukon

1 Jargon of thieves.   A . . . .
2 Rod-shaped.   B . . . .
3 Light rowing boat.   C . . . . .
4 Lover of the fine arts.   D . . . .
5 Spiritless.   E . . . .
6 Sweet dish made with milk,
flour, eggs and honey.   F . . . .
7 Spanish cold vegetable soup.   G azpacho
8 Muhammad's flight from
Mecca.   H . . . . .
9 Caligula's favourite horse.   I . . . .
10 Who wrote *Ulysses*?   J oyce
11 Ornamental loop in yarn.   K . . .
12 Perennial herb.   L . . . .
13 Yielding honey.   M . . . .
14 Indian exhibition of dancing.   N . . . . .
15 Group of eight.   O . . . .
16 Of or like a peacock.   P . . . .
17 Curl plastered down onto
forehead.   Q uiff
18 Beer saloon in a basement.   R . . . .
19 Cavalry saddle cloth.   S . . . .
20 Club foot.   T . . . . . .
21 Greasy.   U . . . .
22 Creamy soup of leeks and
potatoes.   V ichyssoise
23 Dingo dog.   W . . . .
24 Mexican revolutionary
assassinated in 1919.   Z . . . . .

EIGHTY-SEVEN

1   Germanic tribe who invaded England in 5th Century.

A *ngles*

2   What does an apiphobe fear?

B *ees*

3   Musical term 'in a singing style.'

C . . . .

4   Second husband of Mary Queen of Scots.

D *arnley*

5   The art or system of rhythmic movement.

E . . . .

6   A person employed to do all kinds of work.

F . . . .

7   Garden of west slope of Mount of Olives.

G *ethsemane*

8   The science of water.

H *ydralogy*

9   Japanese art of flower arrangement.

I . . . . . .

10   City of Spain famous for producing sherry.

J *erez*

11   Who wrote the poem *The White Man's Burden*?

K *ipling*

12   A butterfly-collector.

L . . . .

13   Woolly, guereza and vervet are types of what?

M . . . . .

14   Belief in nothing.

N . . . .

15   Ugandan president after overthrow of Idi Amin.

O . . . .

16   Famous victory of Clive of India.

P . . . . . .

17   A square dance for four couples.

Q . . . . ,

18   English lexicographer known for his *Thesaurus of English Words and Phrases*.

R *oget*

19   Ur of the Chaldees, early home of Abraham, was the centre of which civilisation?

S *umerian*

20   What lake, partly in Bolivia and partly in Peru, is 12,507 feet above sea level?

T . . . .

21   To present a rolling appearance, like waves.

U . . . . . .

22   Ruling family of Milan from 1277 to 1447.

V . . . .

23   In 1829 the first Oxford v Cambridge boat race took place between Eton and where?

W . . . .

24   Swiss resort at foot of Matterhorn.

Z . . . . . .

EIGHTY-EIGHT

1   Living in trees.

A *rboreal*

2   Marshy offshoot of river in southern America.

B . . . .

3   Set of steam whistles producing musical notes.

C . . . .

4   Wearing low-necked garment.

D . . . .

5   Voice production.

E . . . .

6   With conical or tapering outline.

F . . . .

7   Small German inn.

G . . . .

8   Windspeed over 72 mph.

H *urricane*

9   Capital of Indiana.

I *ndianapolis*

10   Reddish-orange gem.

J . . . . . .

111

11 Traditional Japanese drama.   K *abuki*

12 Of tears.   L *achrymal*

13 Teacher of mystical doctrines.   M . . . .

14 Study of the clouds.   N . . . .

15 Broad sash worn by Japanese.   O . .

16 Golden or cream-coloured horse.   P . . . . . .

17 Fourteen-line poem.   Q . . . .

18 Ornamental screen at back of the altar.   R *eredos*

19 Framework of an organ or cell.   S . . . . . .

20 Cap-like fez.   T *arboosh*

21 Natural pigment, dark-brown.   U . . . . .

22 Having many or very marked veins.   V . . . . .

23 Group of snipe.   W . . .

24 What is the correct name for the 'Isle of Cloves'?   Z . . . .

EIGHTY-NINE

1 Author of *Mansfield Park*.   A *usten*

2 What do you fear if you suffer from bibliophobia?   B *ooks*

3 Currency unit of Brazil.   C . . . .

4 Small freshwater fish of carp family.   D . . .

5 Friendly agreement or relationship between states.   E *ntente*

6   Island group of Denmark in North Atlantic.   F aeroes.

7   An off-breaking ball in cricket, with an apparent leg-break action.   G oogly

8   Castle near Edenbridge in Kent which was the home of Anne Boleyn.   H . . . .

9   Kind of gelatine prepared from the swimming bladder of fishes.   I . . . .

10   The sidepiece or post of a door.   J . . .

11   Jerome K. Jerome – what does the 'K' stand for?   K . . . . .

12   What French province in N America did Napolean sell to the United States in 1803?   L ouisiana

13   Which wine-growing region produces the wines Bernkastel and Piesporter?   M osel

14   Annual plant, sometimes known as the tobacco plant.   N . . . .

15   A kiln to dry hops or malt.   O . . .

16   A solid formation of ancient Greek heavy-armed infantry.   P halynx

17   A stone handmill.   Q uern

18   German airman, better known as the Red Baron.   R ichthofen

19   Currency unit of Tanzania.   S hilling

20   Lowest layer of Earth's atmosphere.   T . . . .

20   Explicit, clear and emphatic.   U nambiguous

22   Change from one state to another.   V olatility.

23   Funnel-shaped, rotating
cloud caused by a tornado at sea.   W . . . .

24   The west wind.   Z *ephyr*

NINETY

1   Snake-like.   A . . . . . .
2   Outer defence of city or castle.   B . . . .
3   Thin, hooded windproof
garment.   C *agoule*
4   Member of Indian armed
robber band.   D *acoit*
5   Drain of blood.   E . . . .
6   Development of bishop across
long diagonal in chess.   F . . . .
7   Roof like a mansard but with
gable ends.   G . . . . . .
8   Short, light, capricious
composition.   H . . . .
9   Drawing of the ground plan of
a building.   I . . . .
10   Ornamental pot or stand for
showing flowers.   J . . . .
11   Rich Indian embroidered
fabric.   K . . . . .
12   Of or like hares.   L *eporine*
13   American organ.   M . . . .
14   Inhabitant of Naples.   N *eapolitan*
15   Surpass in cunning.   O . . . . .
16   Examine by touch.   P . . . . . .
17   Lasting forty days.   Q . . . .
18   Proceeding from a branch.   R . . . .

19 Moaning, whistling, as of wind through the trees.

S . . . .

20 Flooring material of stone chips.

T . . . .

21 Vivid blue colour.

U l t r a m a r i n e

22 Whirling, vortical.

V . . . .

23 On which night do witches gather?

W . . . .

24 Man holding a small landed estate.

Y eoman

NINETY-ONE

1 French philosopher and lover of Héloïse.

A belard

2 What was the name of Alexander the Great's favourite horse?

B . . . .

3 Coiled snailshell-like tube in the ear.

C . . . . . .

4 A stupid person.

D . . . .

5 The ant.

E . . . .

6 Region of SW Belgium and NE France.

F Landers

7 Who was the inventor of printing?

G utenburg

8 What are anise, burnet and hyssop?

H erbs

9 Scene of French and British victory over Russians in Crimean War (1854).

I . . . .

10 Bay which is an inlet of Tasman Sea in SE Australia.

J . . . . .

11 Small two-masted vessel.   K . . . .

12 Wolf-like.   L . . . . .

13 Figure of mis-speech e.g.
'hoist by his own leotard'.   M *alapropism*

14 Scottish mathematician
(1550–1617) who invented
logarithms.   N . . . . .

15 The art of paper folding.   O *rigami*

16 Strait which lies between
India and Sri Lanka.   P . . .

17 Group of mammals with four
feet that can be used as hands.   Q *uadrumana*

18 German diplomat who was
foreign minister from 1938–45.   R . . . .

19 Czech composer of *The
Bartered Bride*.   S . . . . .

20 Minor noble of Anglo-Saxon
times.   T *hane*

21 Region of central Italy.   U *mbria*

22 The greenish rust of copper,
brass or bronze.   V . . . .

23 Pretender to English throne
hanged at Tyburn 1499.   W *arbeck*

24 Any animal which resembles
a plant, e.g. sea anemone.   Z . . . .

NINETY-TWO

1   Devotee of bull fighting.   A . . . .

2   Style of type.   B . . . .

3   Gem polished but not faceted.   C . . . . . .

4   Group of hares.   D . . .

5 What is the name of Sicily's volcano?   E *tna*

6 What is a group of woodcock?   F . . . . .

7 Of the gums.   G . . . .

8 A form of government formed entirely of priests.   H . . . .

9 The Egyptian mongoose known as Pharoah's rat.   I . . . .

10 Name the religious order founded in 1534 by Ignatius Loyola.   J *esuits*

11 What is the most brightly coloured of British birds?   K . . . .

12 What is magnetic iron ore?   L *oadstone*

13 Offspring of black and white persons.   M . . . . . .

14 Territory named South West Africa until 1968.   N *amibia*

15 Yielding oil.   O . . . .

16 Temple dedicated to all of the gods.   P *antheon*

17 Portion.   Q . . . . . .

18 Provençal stew of vegetables.   R *atatouille*

19 In heraldry what is black?   S *able*

20 Woman's apartment.   T . . . .

21 Edible offal of deer.   U . . . . .

22 Church official.   V . . . . .

23 What is a carcajou?   W . . . .

24 The Pope's skullcap.   Z . . . .

NINETY-THREE

1 What was the language of Jesus?

A *ramaic*

2 Into which sea does the River Yukon flow?

B *ering*

3 Greenish-yellow, suffocating gas.

C *hlorine*

4 Famous series of stories written by Boccaccio (1313–75).

D . . . .

5 British psychologist who believes in the absolute measurability of intelligence.

E . . . . . .

6 Brass instrument with three valves and producing mellow sound.

F . . . .

7 A small cucumber used for pickling.

G . . . . . .

8 Liquid measure of 52½ imperial gallons.

H . . . .

9 Chief river of Burma.

I *rrawaddy*

10 Real surname of British Nazi propagandist Lord Haw-haw.

J *oyce*

11 Dish made with fish and rice.

K *edgeree*

12 A book of the words of an opera or a musical.

L *ibretto*

13 French revolutionary stabbed to death in his bath by Charlotte Corday.

M . . . .

14 Historical book of Old Testament.

N *ehimiah*

15 The description of mountains.

O . . . .

118

16   What was first used by a 16th-century Venetian printer, Aldus Manutius?   P . . . .

17   Tropical American tree, the wood of which contains a bitter substance.   Q . . . . .

18   Capital of Morocco.   R *abat*

19   A pot-holer.   S . . . .

20   Indian bandits who strangled or poisoned their victims.   T *hugs*

21   Hooked-shaped.   U . . . .

22   Relating to the fox.   V . . . . .

23   German composer of *Siegfried*.   W *agner*

24   Currency unit of Poland.   Z *loty*

NINETY-FOUR

1   Descent of steep rock face by using double rope.   A *bseil*

2   Half-penny.   B . . . . .

3   Group of goldfinches.   C . . . .

4   Name given to the refuse of molten metal.   D . . . .

5   Lighthouse off the coast of Cornwall.   E . . . .

6   What is page numbering called?   F . . . .

7   Small soldiers from the mountains of Nepal.   G *harkas*

8   Goat-like.   H . . . . . .

9   Sleeplessness.   I *nsomnia*

10   Kingston is the capital of which island?   J *amaica*

11 Old English name for hemlock. K . .

12 Ship of Chinese rig but European shape. L . . . . .

13 Astringent plum-like fruit. M . . . .

14 Famous Russian ballet dancer. N *ijinski*

15 Servile. O . . . .

16 Of a marsh. P . . . . . .

17 Central American bird. Q . . . . .

18 Directed backwards. R . . . .

19 Person affected with scurvy. S . . . .

20 American larch. T . . . . . .

21 Last syllable of a word. U *ltima*

22 South African Prime Minister assassinated in 1966. V . . . .

23 Lord Chancellor of England's seat in the House of Lords. W *oolsack*

24 Large unspecified number. Z *illion*

NINETY-FIVE
_____

1 Capital of Paraguay. A *suncion*

2 Inventor of a process for making steel. B . . . .

3 Who was chief conspirator in the Gunpowder Plot? C *atesby*

4 Who was Don Quixote's lady love? D *ulcinea*

5 The science of investigation of the derivation and original meaning of words. E *tymology*

6 What word comes from the Portuguese 'feitico' meaning sorcery?

F . . . . .

7 English novelist whose best known work is *Lord of the Flies*.

G olding

8 One of four main islands of Japan.

H onshu

9 Ancient British tribe who revolted under their queen Boadicea.

I ceni

10 What was the name of the mother of Oedipus?

J ocasta

11 Variety of cabbage with curly leaves.

K . . .

12 Battle fought on 7 October 1571 between the fleets of Austria, Italy and Spain and the fleet of Turkey.

L epanto

13 Who, in 1840, invented the first bicycle with pedals?

M acmillan

14 Want of knowledge.

N . . . .

15 American physicist whose research led to production of atomic bomb.

O ppenheimer

16 An ancient British supreme chief.

P . . . .

17 An arrangement of five things, like pips on a domino.

Q . . .

18 The killing of a king.

R egicide

19 What have upright centre pins called gnomens?

S undials

20 An ancient musical instrument carried in the hand.

T . . . . . .

21 In Swahili it means freedom and it is the new name for Mt Kilimanjaro.   U . . . .

22 Dynasty of French kings.   V a l o i s

23 North American elk.   W a p i t i

24 A fossil animal.   Z . . . . . .

NINETY-SIX

1 The citadel of ancient Athens.   A c r o p o l i s

2 Soft alloy of tin, antimony, copper and lead.   B . . . . .

3 Peace pipe.   C . . . . . .

4 Group of lapwings.   D . . . . .

5 Imaginary region of S America abounding in gold.   E l d o r a d o

6 Painting on plastered walls with special pigments.   F r e s c o

7 Marijuana.   G . . . .

8 Hawker.   H . . . . . .

9 Stain with blood.   I . . . . .

10 German or Austrian rifleman.   J . . . . .

11 Double-handled cup used in ancient Greece.   K . . . .

12 A kind of Turkish tobacco.   L . . . . . .

13 Cold wind that sweeps over France and N Italy.   M . . . . . .

14 Satellite of Neptune.   N e r e i d

15 The leading timber state of USA.   O r e g o n

16 Drum roll with alternate beating of sticks.   P . . . .

17   Daily.   Q *uotidian*

18   Snake akin to a cobra.   R . . . .

19   Which country is known as
Helvetia?   S *witzerland*

20   Sweetmeat like toffee.   T . . . .

21   Being excessively fond of
one's wife.   U . . . .

22   In which country is
Maracaibo?   V *enezuela*

23   Four-stroke rotary internal-
combustion engine.   W . . . . .

24   Brute in human shape.   Y . . . .

NINETY-SEVEN

1   Bay where Nelson destroyed
the French fleet in 1798.   A *boukir*

2   For what, in the reign of Charles
II, did Frances Stewart model?   B . . . .

3   What port is at the Atlantic
end of the Panama Canal?   C *olon*

4   Currency unit of Greece.   D *rachma*

5   In 1827 who worked on the
Communist Manifesto with Karl
Marx?   E *ngels*

6   French general who was Allied
Supreme Commander (1918).   F *och*

7   English author whose works
include *I, Claudius*.   G *raves*

8   Greek historian known as the
father of history.   H *erodotus*

9   Peninsular of N W Yugoslavia
in Adriatic Sea.   I *stria*

10   Being placed together.   J *uxtaposed*

11   What is epistemology the
theory of?   K *nowledge*

12   French cinema pioneer who,
with his brother, invented the
cinematograph.   L . . . . . .

13   Which poet was killed in a
tavern brawl aged twenty-nine?   M *arlow*

14   Pertaining to swimming.   N . . . .

15   Figure of speech e.g. 'cruel to
be kind'.   O . . . .

16   A pound or enclosure for
cattle.   P . . . . . .

17   Fifth power of a million.   Q *uadrillion*

18   Transfer forces, workers from
one area to another.   R . . . .

19   What are peccatophobes
afraid of?   S *inning*

20   The science of poisons.   T *oxicology*

21   Town of S W Germany on
River Danube.   U *lm*

22   Brazilian statesman, president
1930–45 and 1951–4.   V . . . . .

23   Genus of climbing shrubs of
leguminosae family.   W *isteria*

24   A camp protected by a
stockade.   Z . . . . .

NINETY-EIGHT

1   The third brightest star visible
in the northern hemisphere.   A . . . .

2   Light steel helmet.   B . . . . . .

3 Group of choughs.

C . . . .

4 First portion of stomach.

D uodenum

5 Who was known as the 'king of chips'?

E . . . .

6 Orange-brown British butterflies.

F . . . .

7 Noah's ark was supposedly made of the wood of this tree.

G opher

8 Fabulous griffin-like creature with body of a horse.

H ippogriff

9 Chink.

I . . . .

10 Waggish.

J . . . . .

11 Iron-hoisting bucket in mines.

K . . . . .

12 What is the lightest metal?

L . . . . . .

13 Extinct flightless bird.

M . .

14 Later period of the Stone Age.

N eolithic

15 Relating to the eye.

O . . . .

16 Saddle horse for easy riding.

P alfrey

17 Hut similar to nissen.

Q . . . . . .

18 Group of martens.

R . . . . . .

19 Capital of Bulgaria.

S ofia

20 Connected with the sense of touch.

T actile

21 Homosexual.

U . . . . .

22 Largest lake in Africa.

V ictoria

23 Married state.

W edlock

24 Cards used in ESP experiments.

Z ener

NINETY-NINE

1   What river is crossed in Florence by the Ponte Vecchio?

A Arno

2   Where was the land speed record broken sixteen times from 1935–70?

B . . . .

3   Curve formed by chain hanging from two fixed points.

C atenary

4   Combination of two vowels into a single sound.

D iphthong

5   Study and classification of insects.

E . . . .

6   Archbishop of Canterbury 1945–61.

F isher

7   State of western India.

G ujarat

8   A South African antelope.

H artebeest

9   The science of fossil footprints.

I . . . .

10   Which eight-foot giant, who died 1798, was buried in the Bank of England?

J . . . . . .

11   Species of phosphorescent shrimps.

K . . . .

12   Knight of German legend whose story is basis of Wagner opera.

L ohengrin

13   Figure of speech where the name of one thing is put for another e.g. 'the bottle' for 'drink'.

M . . . .

14   Asiatic pygmies are called negrites, what are African pygmies called?

N egrilles

15   Rare mammal of giraffe family.

O kapi

16 The study of seaweeds. P . . . .

17 Currency unit of Guatemala. Q *uetzal*

18 Puzzle where a word, name or phrase is represented by pictures or signs. R . . . .

19 Province of eastern China on the Yellow Sea. S *handong*

20 What was the scavenger's daughter used for? T . . . . . .

21 The second largest lake in England. U *llswater*

22 Archipelago of S W Pacific Ocean, formerly New Hebrides. V *anuatu*

23 The Tower of London has thirteen inner towers. Which one contains the Crown Jewels? W *akefield*

24 The art of engraving on wood. X *ylography*

ONE HUNDRED

1 Roman Catholic prayer said at 6 a.m., noon, 6 p.m. A . . . . . .

2 Cellar or shop selling wine. B . . . . .

3 Group of cats. C . . . . . .

4 Group of sheldrake. D . . . . . .

5 Fit for food. E . . . .

6 Number series 0–1–1–2–3–5–8. F . . . .

7 Bush or small tree, related to plum. G . . . .

8 Another name for daddy-long-legs. H . . . .

9 Animal living in home of another.   I . . . .

10 Aquatic invertebrate.   J . . . .

11 Instrument for recording pressure.   K . . . .

12 Reading desk.   L . . . . . .

13 Ulan Bator is the capital of which country?   M . . . .

14 Nonexistence.   N . . . .

15 Darken.   O . . . .

16 Small palm tree.   P . . . .

17 Star-like object with red shift.   Q . . . . .

18 Red ochre.   R . . . . .

19 With short stiff hairs.   S . . . .

20 Head of foreign business in China.   T . . . . .

21 Sacred serpent.   U . . . . .

22 Caprice.   V . . . . .

23 Winged two-legged dragon.   W . . . . .

24 Humped ox.   Z . . .

128

Solutions

ONE

1 Astrology 2 Bushel 3 Countess 4 Dingo 5 Ermine
6 Freezing 7 Gunpowder 8 Heat 9 Independence 10 James
11 Kremlin 12 Legion 13 Micawber 14 Nostalgia
15 Octopus 16 Pancakes 17 Quoits 18 Richard 19 Singer
20 Tomahawk 21 Utopia 22 Victoria 23 Whittington
24 Yodel

10–12	Fair
13–17	Good
18–21	Very good
22–24	Excellent

TWO

1 Ambrosia 2 Biped 3 Campus 4 Divot 5 Ear 6 Faggot
7 Guzzle 8 Honeydew 9 Igloo 10 Jaffa 11 Kink 12 Lava
13 Mansion 14 Nylon 15 Ooze 16 Parasol 17 Quack
18 Ruby 19 Skulk 20 Team 21 Ulcer 22 Veal
23 Worship 24 Yacht

10–12	Fair
13–17	Good
18–21	Very good
22–24	Excellent

THREE

1 Aldaniti 2 Ballot 3 Cartoon 4 Decibel 5 Edelweiss
6 Fonteyn 7 Gosling 8 Hydrogen 9 Imposter 10 Jerico
11 Koran 12 Lasso 13 Mercury 14 Nicholas 15 Orleans
16 Philately 17 Quartet 18 Raleigh 19 Social
20 Thunderer 21 Ulysses 22 Velvet 23 White 24 Yokel

10–12	Fair
13–17	Good
18–21	Very good
22–24	Excellent

FOUR

1 Amazons 2 Baboon 3 Calico 4 Dodo 5 Ewe 6 Facet
7 Gusto 8 Harvester 9 Imp 10 Jive 11 Keg 12 Lion
13 Madrid 14 Noon 15 Orb 16 Pastor 17 Quaff
18 Rasher 19 Siesta 20 Tusk 21 Urn 22 Varlet
23 Wallet 24 Zinc

10–12	Fair
13–17	Good
18–21	Very good
22–24	Excellent

FIVE

1 Alkalis 2 Boiler 3 Cabinet 4 Diamond 5 Evaporation
6 Four 7 Geisha 8 Horticulture 9 Isosceles 10 Jamboree
11 Knock 12 Liberty 13 Monaco 14 Nucleus 15 Orwell
16 Pentagram 17 Quorum 18 Raspberry 19 Shakespeare
20 Tutankhamen 21 Ultimo 22 Volume 23 Woolsack
24 X-ray

10–12	Fair
13–17	Good
18–21	Very good
22–24	Excellent

SIX

1 Arizona 2 Bedlam 3 Caber 4 Dobbin 5 Edit 6 Forte
7 Gateau 8 Hornpipe 9 Icon 10 Jape 11 Knuckle
12 Lathe 13 Minstrel 14 Neddy 15 Ogre 16 Papal
17 Queen 18 Roc 19 Stamina 20 Toreador 21 Upset
22 Villa 23 Wine 24 Yen

10–12	Fair
13–17	Good
18–21	Very good
22–24	Excellent

SEVEN

1 America 2 Bat 3 Chemistry 4 Direct 5 Éclair
6 Frankenstein 7 Guinea 8 Halloween 9 Illusion 10 James
11 Knot 12 Leasehold 13 Marquis 14 Nassau 15 Oyster
16 Puccini 17 Quadruped 18 Rasputin 19 Stonewall
20 Tarot 21 Ukelele 22 Vitamins 23 Wrestling 24 Yellow

10–12	Fair
13–16	Good
17–20	Very good
21–24	Excellent

EIGHT

1 Amazon 2 Belfry 3 Cache 4 Dinghy 5 Elope 6 Felon
7 Gazump 8 Hookah 9 Innards 10 Javelin 11 Kite
12 Labrador 13 Mikado 14 Nook 15 Oasis 16 Pallet
17 Quest 18 Ranee 19 Sprite 20 Tango 21 Umpteen
22 Valance 23 Wheat 24 Yak

10–12	Fair
13–16	Good
17–20	Very good
21–24	Excellent

NINE

1 Amman 2 Bounty 3 Census 4 Dumpling 5 Economics
6 Florence 7 Geology 8 Heifer 9 Imminent 10 Jefferson
11 Khrushchev 12 Linen 13 Mandarin 14 Novel
15 Overture 16 Poe 17 Quarantine 18 Recorder
19 Silverstone 20 Twain 21 Udder 22 Viper 23 Watt
24 Young

10–12	Fair
13–16	Good
17–20	Very good
21–24	Excellent

TEN

1 Abacus 2 Berne 3 Canasta 4 Dicky 5 Eddy 6 Facia
7 Guru 8 Howdah 9 Interim 10 Janitor 11 Kennel
12 Limbo 13 Musket 14 Negligee 15 Onus 16 Patriot
17 Quail 18 Rivulet 19 Scrim 20 Troy 21 Usher
22 Valeta 23 Wizard 24 Yam

10–12	Fair
13–16	Good
17–20	Very good
21–24	Excellent

ELEVEN

1 Annuals 2 Blackbeard 3 China 4 Dialect
5 Equestrianism 6 Freud 7 Geyser 8 Hornet 9 Impresario
10 Jehovah 11 Kebab 12 Logic 13 Maritime 14 Novello
15 Omelette 16 Perjury 17 Queensbury 18 Ramadan
19 Shaw 20 Trinder 21 Umbrella 22 Vulgar 23 Whippet
24 Yeomen

9–11	Fair
12–15	Good
16–19	Very good
20–24	Excellent

TWELVE

1 Alpha 2 Ballerina 3 Carafe 4 Dirk 5 Elite 6 Flapjack
7 Garnet 8 Halibut 9 Ibex 10 Jerkin 11 Kiosk
12 Lassitude 13 Mirage 14 Noodles 15 Oof 16 Paragon
17 Quarrel 18 Regatta 19 Stomp 20 Tuba 21 Umpire
22 Vassal 23 Wholly 24 Zany

 9–11   Fair
12–15   Good
16–19   Very good
20–24   Excellent

THIRTEEN

1 Arkansas 2 Bakelite 3 Columbus 4 Deciduous
5 Equilibrium 6 Fields 7 Ganges 8 Holst 9 Incas 10 Juliet
11 Krakatoa 12 Lawrence 13 Mandolin 14 Nimble
15 Orienteering 16 Palladium 17 Quandary 18 Romany
19 Sousa 20 Tureen 21 Urchin 22 Vacuum 23 Wren
24 Yeti

 9–11   Fair
12–15   Good
16–19   Very good
20–24   Excellent

FOURTEEN

1 Albumen 2 Bedaub 3 Cabal 4 Dinosaur 5 Ember
6 Flotilla 7 Gondola 8 Haberdasher 9 Iguana 10 Jiffy
11 Knight 12 Leeward 13 Muslin 14 Nomad 15 Oomph
16 Papoose 17 Quadruplet 18 Rodeo 19 Supersede
20 Tripod 21 Umbrage 22 Vixen 23 Wrist 24 Yucca

 9–11   Fair
12–15   Good
16–19   Very good
20–24   Excellent

FIFTEEN

1 Aqueduct 2 Buffalo 3 Cannabis 4 Dunlop 5 Estuary
6 Flamingo 7 Greig 8 Hardy 9 Incubation 10 Jobber
11 Karate 12 Livingstone 13 Mecca 14 National 15 Oboe
16 Pampas 17 Quebec 18 Rack 19 Sane 20 Testator
21 Uganda 22 Valentino 23 Wafer 24 Zither

9–11	Fair
12–15	Good
16–19	Very good
20–24	Excellent

SIXTEEN

1 Alpenhorn 2 Besom 3 Carousel 4 Dhobi 5 Encounter
6 Filbert 7 Gyve 8 Hara-kiri 9 Inebriate 10 Jesus
11 Kangaroo 12 Liberate 13 Masquerade 14 Noose
15 Orchard 16 Palliasse 17 Quibble 18 Russet
19 Squabble 20 Tuxedo 21 Utter 22 Vernal 23 Whirl
24 York

9–11	Fair
12–15	Good
16–19	Very good
20–24	Excellent

SEVENTEEN

1 Apache 2 Barometer 3 Cupid 4 Damascus 5 Egypt
6 Flux 7 Grant 8 Hamper 9 Incognito 10 Jemmy
11 Kidd 12 Leonardo 13 Masefield 14 Ness 15 Otter
16 Portia 17 Quakers 18 Rayon 19 Sprat 20 Teal
21 Universe 22 Vampire 23 Waterloo 24 Zucchini

9–11	Fair
12–14	Good
15–18	Very good
19–24	Excellent

134

EIGHTEEN

1 Alpenstock 2 Balustrade 3 Cabaret 4 Doggo 5 Edible
6 Facade 7 Goulash 8 Harridan 9 Identikit 10 Jade
11 Knapsack 12 Layette 13 Membrane 14 Nausea
15 Oodles 16 Paling 17 Quoin 18 Rancid 19 Sombrero
20 Talon 21 Unison 22 Vaudeville 23 Witch
24 Xylophone

9–11	Fair
12–14	Good
15–18	Very good
19–24	Excellent

NINETEEN

1 Androcles 2 Brass 3 Cheeky 4 Delphi 5 Exmoor
6 Farouk 7 Georgetown 8 Hovercraft 9 Incinerator
10 Jekyll 11 Kaiser 12 Labyrinth 13 Milton 14 Napkin
15 Ohio 16 Piebald 17 Quire 18 Rhine 19 Shepard
20 Tutu 21 Under 22 Velocity 23 Wayne 24 Zigzag

9–11	Fair
12–14	Good
15–18	Very good
19–24	Excellent

TWENTY

1 Abattoir 2 Ballyhoo 3 Cairn 4 Dachshund 5 Easel
6 Fledgling 7 Galahad 8 Hickory 9 Impi 10 Jonah
11 Kinship 12 Locusts 13 Mondial 14 North-easter
15 Ostrich 16 Paté 17 Quasimodo 18 Rotund 19 Snippet
20 Tulle 21 Uncle 22 Valentine 23 Waltz 24 Zero

9–11	Fair
12–14	Good
15–18	Very good
19–24	Excellent

TWENTY-ONE

1 Aphrodite 2 Burlesque 3 Colorado 4 Democracy 5 Enlist
6 Fence 7 Gorse 8 Haddock 9 Impound 10 Jaywalker
11 Kaunda 12 Lizard 13 Methane 14 Nawab 15 Obesity
16 Pawnee 17 Quicksilver 18 Romans 19 Styx
20 Truman 21 Unicorn 22 Valparaiso 23 Wellesley
24 Yashmak

8–10	Fair
11–13	Good
14–17	Very good
18–24	Excellent

TWENTY-TWO

1 Africa 2 Beta 3 Cassowary 4 Decimal 5 Eager
6 Flambeau 7 Gizzard 8 Harbinger 9 Imbibe 10 Jury
11 Ketchup 12 Lobelia 13 Mentor 14 Novice 15 Otter
16 Pasture 17 Quango 18 Rumba 19 Sedate 20 Tussock
21 Underskirt 22 Vamoose 23 Wedding 24 Zebra

8–10	Fair
11–13	Good
14–17	Very good
18–24	Excellent

TWENTY-THREE

1 Albania 2 Babylon 3 Cuba 4 Dynamo 5 Eider 6 Fellow
7 Garland 8 Hectare 9 Importune 10 Jackpot
11 Kamikaze 12 Longfellow 13 Mozart 14 Newfoundland
15 Octahedron 16 Parchment 17 Quagmire 18 Rupee
19 Steppes 20 Tintinnabulation 21 Unfathomable
22 Vertebrates 23 Wells 24 Zeppelin

8–10	Fair
11–13	Good
14–17	Very good
18–24	Excellent

TWENTY-FOUR

1 Alpaca 2 Bidet 3 Caboodle 4 Disco 5 Expire 6 Fiesta
7 Garbo 8 Hacienda 9 Incense 10 Jankers 11 Knead
12 Ligament 13 Menagerie 14 Nashville 15 Ottoman
16 Parakeet 17 Quickstep 18 Rustic 19 Sanctity
20 Tantrum 21 Upswept 22 Vermicelli 23 Wallet 24 Yew

8–10	Fair
11–13	Good
14–17	Very good
18–24	Excellent

TWENTY-FIVE

1 Alliteration 2 Bastille 3 Charlie 4 Deltas 5 Edison
6 Frequency 7 Gymnastics 8 Holland 9 Immunity
10 Jerome 11 Knickerbockers 12 Lenin 13 Macbeth
14 Napoleon 15 Oblique 16 Peseta 17 Quiver
18 Redwood 19 Sofia 20 Tsetse 21 University 22 Verona
23 Watling 24 Yorker

8–10	Fair
11–13	Good
14–17	Very good
18–24	Excellent

TWENTY-SIX

1 Actuary 2 Backgammon 3 Cerise 4 Doggerel 5 Estimate
6 Flamenco 7 Gargoyle 8 Hoggin 9 Idiom 10 Jerk
11 Kestrel 12 Lurid 13 Manitoba 14 Numskull 15 Ostrich
16 Paragraph 17 Quadragesima 18 Rook 19 Scintillate
20 Trite 21 Urals 22 Vacillate 23 Whitlow 24 Yedo

8–10	Fair
11–13	Good
14–17	Very good
18–24	Excellent

TWENTY-SEVEN

1 Andante   2 Biology   3 Centaur   4 Disraeli   5 Eliot
6 Freetown   7 Gravitation   8 Hormuz   9 Iris   10 Jerusalem
11 Keaton   12 Lammas   13 Molluscs   14 Narcissus
15 Oratorio   16 Priestley   17 Quirk   18 Russell
19 Spoonerism   20 Trombone   21 Unique   22 Victor
23 Walton   24 Yemen

 8–10   Fair
11–13   Good
14–17   Very good
18–24   Excellent

TWENTY-EIGHT

1 Acupuncture   2 Bagatelle   3 Clavicle   4 Dragon
5 Escalator   6 Flotsam   7 Garrotte   8 Hoi polloi   9 Incisors
10 Jaguar   11 Kiln   12 Lent   13 Metatarsus   14 Novelette
15 Oslo   16 Pasta   17 Quinsy   18 Ramshackle   19 Synopsis
20 Tarantula   21 Utopia   22 Veldt   23 Wren   24 Yugoslav

 8–10   Fair
11–13   Good
14–17   Very good
18–24   Excellent

TWENTY-NINE

1 Albino   2 Bisley   3 Caviare   4 Dominoes   5 Esperanto
6 Franklin   7 Gilbert   8 Humus   9 Integer   10 Johannesburg
11 Kibbutz   12 Laughing   13 Monrovia   14 Niagara
15 Oscar   16 Perennials   17 Quaich   18 Ragtime
19 Scalene   20 Telford   21 Undergraduate   22 Vestals
23 Wanderlust   24 Zeppo

 8–10   Fair
11–13   Good
14–17   Very good
18–24   Excellent

THIRTY

1 Akimbo 2 Bistro 3 Coliseum 4 Decathlon 5 Expert
6 Flagellants 7 Gaberdine 8 Heavyside 9 Ingle-nook
10 Janus 11 Khaki 12 Lackey 13 Martingale 14 Nitwit
15 Orange 16 Panorama 17 Quid 18 Ray 19 Scrutiny
20 Twaddle 21 Uric 22 Volery 23 Wales 24 Zeal

8–10	Fair
11–13	Good
14–17	Very good
18–24	Excellent

THIRTY-ONE

1 Alluvium 2 Bison 3 Cacti 4 Doldrums 5 Entirely
6 Frank 7 Grizzly 8 Hope 9 Instability 10 Judo 11 Kabul
12 Lewis 13 Mafeking 14 Nobel 15 Ornithology
16 Pewter 17 Quaint 18 Riposte 19 Saladin 20 Titanic
21 Underwriter 22 Victoria 23 Whisky 24 Zenith

7–9	Fair
10–12	Good
13–16	Very good
17–24	Excellent

THIRTY-TWO

1 Adze 2 Blunderbuss 3 Caballero 4 Dhow 5 Elan
6 Foxglove 7 Gambit 8 Houdini 9 Isis 10 Jaundice
11 Klondike 12 Lagoon 13 Moussaka 14 Nincompoop
15 Ocarina 16 Panzers 17 Quidnunc 18 Rattlesnake
19 Shovel-board 20 Trellis 21 Unkindness 22 Victoria
23 Wedge 24 Zoom

7–9	Fair
10–12	Good
13–16	Very good
17–24	Excellent

THIRTY-THREE

1 Anchovy 2 Botany 3 Chimpanzee 4 Dickens 5 Ebony
6 Flying 7 Garrick 8 Hansard 9 Ironsides 10 Jinx
11 Kowloon 12 Lobster 13 Mildew 14 Newton
15 Omnipotent 16 Pacifism 17 Quarry 18 Rachman
19 Sardinia 20 Troubadour 21 Uptight 22 Valencia
23 Waugh 24 Yankee

7–9	Fair
10–12	Good
13–16	Very good
17–24	Excellent

THIRTY-FOUR

1 Ananas 2 Boutique 3 Cahoots 4 Dipsomaniac 5 Epitaph
6 Ferric 7 Gazelle 8 Hussy 9 Idaho 10 Joey 11 Kris
12 Leotard 13 Mizzen 14 Noxious 15 Octopus
16 Pantechnicon 17 Quiche 18 Rill 19 Symphony
20 Thermos 21 Uruguay 22 Viking 23 Whet 24 Yippee

7–9	Fair
10–12	Good
13–16	Very good
17–24	Excellent

THIRTY-FIVE

1 Anastasia 2 Blood 3 Chartwell 4 Darwin 5 Ecology
6 Farrier 7 Gyroscope 8 Hapsburgs 9 Ibsen 10 Java
11 Kelp 12 Lepidoptera 13 Mesopotamia 14 Noggin
15 Optics 16 Plimsoll 17 Quaver 18 Ravioli
29 Seismograph 20 Trinidad 21 Ugli 22 Valletta
23 Wisley 24 Xenon

7–9	Fair
10–12	Good
13–16	Very good
17–24	Excellent

THIRTY-SIX

1 Albert 2 Bobbin 3 Caisson 4 Demijohn 5 Exude 6 Faro
7 Graffiti 8 Hexad 9 Ilex 10 Jonquil 11 Knap 12 Lofter
13 Murine 14 Nubile 15 Onerous 16 Patella 17 Quay
18 Reynard 19 Skedaddle 20 Torso 21 Unguent 22 Veldt
23 Wimple 24 Yoga

7–9	Fair
10–12	Good
13–16	Very good
17–24	Excellent

THIRTY-SEVEN

1 Alhambra 2 Bernstein 3 Cyclone 4 Diana 5 Eligible
6 Fallow 7 Griffith 8 Hargreaves 9 Impeccable 10 Jasmine
11 Knox 12 Lincoln 13 Monopoly 14 Nectarine 15 Ovine
16 Phoenix 17 Questionable 18 Revere 19 Sicily
20 Tennyson 21 Unionist 22 Vermouth 23 Withers
24 Yiddish

7–9	Fair
10–12	Good
13–16	Very good
17–24	Excellent

THIRTY-EIGHT

1 Allegro 2 Bezique 3 Cicada 4 Dirigible 5 Embroil
6 Fiscal 7 Gloaming 8 Halitosis 9 Italic 10 Juggins
11 Kirsch 12 Lariat 13 Mufti 14 Nippon 15 Optic
16 Patio 17 Quill 18 Roseate 19 Stanchion 20 Toledo
21 Ulterior 22 Vitrify 23 Wardship 24 Yarborough

7–9	Fair
10–12	Good
13–16	Very good
17–24	Excellent

THIRTY-NINE

1 Archimedes 2 Basil 3 Catacombs 4 Dixie 5 Eiger
6 Femur 7 Gibbon 8 Hannibal 9 Inkling 10 Jeans
11 Kingsley 12 Lyre 13 Magenta 14 Nostradamus
15 Owens 16 Piccolo 17 Queensland 18 Risqué
19 Solomon 20 Thackeray 21 Uncouth 22 Vivaldi
23 Wildflowers 24 Yosemite

7–9	Fair
10–12	Good
13–16	Very good
17–24	Excellent

FORTY

1 Aplomb 2 Borzoi 3 Calvados 4 Davit 5 Equity
6 Fondue 7 Gaucho 8 Hustings 9 Igneous 10 Julep
11 Kittiwake 12 Laconic 13 Macabre 14 Nuptial
15 Opaque 16 Pecan 17 Queue 18 Riesling 19 Schmuck
20 Triad 21 Umbra 22 Vesta 23 Woggle 24 Zeta

7–9	Fair
10–12	Good
13–16	Very good
17–24	Excellent

FORTY-ONE

1 Achilles 2 Blenheim 3 Cedars 4 Defoe 5 Empire 6 Five
7 Godiva 8 Herringbone 9 Impatiens 10 Jackdaw
11 Keystone 12 Lexicon 13 Magellan 14 Neurology
15 Orinoco 16 Pinza 17 Quota 18 Rouble 19 Stye
20 Tundra 21 Undercover 22 Volgograd 23 Wodehouse
24 Zulu

7–8	Fair
9–12	Good
13–16	Very good
17–24	Excellent

FORTY-TWO

1 Aileron 2 Barbel 3 Caboose 4 Dewlap 5 Erratum
6 Filial 7 Glissade 8 Homily 9 Idyll 10 Jodhpurs
11 Kerchief 12 Logistics 13 Mollify 14 Nuance
15 Occident 16 Paucity 17 Quadrangle 18 Risotto
19 Scapula 20 Tombola 21 Uvula 22 Vernier 23 Waffle
24 Zoology

7–8	Fair
9–12	Good
13–16	Very good
17–24	Excellent

FORTY-THREE

1 Amritsar 2 Begonia 3 Chain 4 Derrick 5 Erin
6 Furniture 7 Gainsborough 8 Huguenots 9 Ionosphere
10 Junk 11 Kissinger 12 Longleat 13 Monroe
14 Nebraska 15 Oman 16 Papyrus 17 Quash 18 Rice
19 Schilling 20 Topiary 21 Ultrasonics 22 Volleyball
23 Wordsworth 24 Xerxes

7–8	Fair
9–12	Good
13–16	Very good
17–24	Excellent

FORTY-FOUR

1 Apollo 2 Baccarat 3 Crenellated 4 Diadem 5 Expound
6 Fletcher 7 Goatee 8 Halma 9 Iota 10 Jargon
11 Krugerand 12 Lugubrious 13 Mambo 14 Niggard
15 Opossum 16 Pedagogue 17 Quixote 18 Roué
19 Spillikin 20 Titanic 21 Unctuous 22 Volant 23 Weevil
24 Yearling

7–8	Fair
9–12	Good
13–16	Very good
17–24	Excellent

FORTY-FIVE

1 Amphibia 2 Bogota 3 Codicil 4 Denmark 5 Exorcism
6 Falsetto 7 Gelatine 8 Hotel 9 Ides 10 Jellicoe
11 Kookaburra 12 Lychgate 13 Micrometer 14 Niblick
15 Offenbach 16 Pizarro 17 Quartermaster 18 Rosette
19 Swastika 20 Tern 21 Urban 22 Valise 23 Warlock
24 Zagreb

7–8	Fair
9–12	Good
13–16	Very good
17–24	Excellent

FORTY-SIX

1 Aperitif 2 Bairn 3 Cayman 4 Delilah 5 Enamour
6 Fetlock 7 Gourmet 8 Hogmanay 9 Ignoramus 10 Jersey
11 Kemp 12 Lasagne 13 Myopia 14 Nocturne 15 Octavo
16 Parquet 17 Quadrant 18 Rickshaw 19 Sampan
20 Tiddly 21 Urbane 22 Verruca 23 Wastrel 24 Zest

7–8	Fair
9–12	Good
13–16	Very good
17–24	Excellent

FORTY-SEVEN

1 Atheism 2 Bumble 3 Carnivores 4 Drone 5 Everglades
6 Fatalism 7 Grimm 8 Head 9 Ignominy 10 Jeffreys
11 Kiel 12 Lemming 13 Medusa 14 Nadir 15 Opium
16 Paderewski 17 Quantum 18 Rodin 19 Sailing
20 Tricolour 21 Ursine 22 Velodrome 23 Waldheim
24 Zambezi

6–8	Fair
9–11	Good
12–15	Very good
16–24	Excellent

144

FORTY-EIGHT

1 Apse   2 Beaufort   3 Caprine   4 Dhoti   5 Espouse
6 Firmament   7 Genuflect   8 Hoplite   9 Iridescent   10 Junket
11 Kowtow   12 Largo   13 Midden   14 Nocturnal   15 Octet
16 Pastoral   17 Quadrillion   18 Rosarium   19 Savannah
20 Tinnitus   21 Ullage   22 Volar   23 Waspish   24 Yoicks

6–8	Fair
9–11	Good
12–15	Very good
16–24	Excellent

FORTY-NINE

1 Augusta   2 Byron   3 Charlemagne   4 Dyslexia   5 Exodus
6 Foinavon   7 Guilder   8 Herculaneum   9 Inert   10 Juliana
11 Khomeini   12 Lucerne   13 Magistrate   14 Napalm
15 Osprey   16 Potassium   17 Quip   18 Rosemary
19 Squeers   20 Tynwald   21 Ubiquity   22 Vulcanization
23 Weir   24 Yokohama

6–8	Fair
9–11	Good
12–15	Very good
16–24	Excellent

FIFTY

1 Apothecary   2 Banshee   3 Cabriolet   4 Decapod   5 Embalm
6 Fedora   7 Gaskin   8 Hoopoe   9 Ivories   10 Jenny
11 Kipper   12 Lancelot   13 Median   14 Nicker   15 Oakum
16 Pauper   17 Quartz   18 Rotavator   19 Sozzled
20 Toxophilite   21 Uppity   22 Vernacular   23 Wanton
24 Xebec

6–8	Fair
9–11	Good
12–15	Very good
16–24	Excellent

FIFTY-ONE

1 Auk 2 Barrie 3 Caesar 4 Dahlia 5 Ewer 6 Fairbanks
7 Guatemala 8 Hedgehog 9 Impressionism 10 Jacobean
11 Kansas 12 Lloyd 13 Memphis 14 Nuffield 15 Octant
16 Pantomime 17 Quaternary 18 Rowan 19 Shinty
20 Theatres 21 Usury 22 Voltaire 23 Waterford
24 Yangtze

6–8	Fair
9–11	Good
12–15	Very good
16–24	Excellent

FIFTY-TWO

1 Arcady 2 Bivouac 3 Cicerone 4 Didicoy 5 Endive
6 Falsetto 7 Gravid 8 Herbivores 9 Ingot 10 Jujube
11 Kaput 12 Lory 13 Maunder 14 Newt 15 Orator
16 Pannikin 17 Quadriceps 18 Rotunda 19 Steenbok
20 Tic 21 Ustinov 22 Voile 23 Waif 24 Yearling

6–8	Fair
9–11	Good
12–15	Very good
16–24	Excellent

FIFTY-THREE

1 Amaryllis 2 Blackmore 3 Carnation 4 Dacca 5 Ennui
6 Ford's 7 Glucose 8 Herschel 9 Isis 10 Jenkins
11 Kelvin 12 Lowry 13 Marsupials 14 Narcissism
15 Oxlip 16 Paradox 17 Quiz 18 Rissole 19 Sidewinder
20 Tunny 21 Uranium 22 Vanbrugh 23 Wirral 24 Ying

6–8	Fair
9–11	Good
12–15	Very good
16–24	Excellent

FIFTY-FOUR

1 Android 2 Bazooka 3 Colubrine 4 Davenport 5 Exquisite
6 Frog 7 Georgio 8 Houris 9 Irascible 10 Joust
11 Kleptomanic 12 Loupe 13 McKinley 14 Nickelodeon
15 Octagon 16 Patisserie 17 Quartan 18 Rexine
19 Sycophant 20 Tattoo 21 Ulna 22 Vol-au-vent
23 Willies 24 Yuan

6–8	Fair
9–11	Good
12–15	Very good
16–24	Excellent

FIFTY-FIVE

1 Azalea 2 Burns 3 Condor 4 Duvalier 5 Eyre 6 Flora
7 Goethe 8 Hairdresser 9 Inner 10 Jujitsu 11 Klaxon
12 Libido 13 Markets 14 Neptune 15 Ombudsman
16 Pierrot 17 Quito 18 Rostrum 19 Skagerrak
20 Tercentenary 21 Ulbricht 22 Vertigo 23 Whitebait
24 Zingaro

6–8	Fair
9–11	Good
12–15	Very good
16–24	Excellent

FIFTY-SIX

1 Advocaat 2 Bagel 3 Clerihew 4 Denarius 5 Effrontery
6 Flunkey 7 Gorgon 8 Hobbledehoy 9 Iberian 10 Jitter
11 Kayak 12 Laudanum 13 Mordant 14 Nacre 15 Occult
16 Pallid 17 Quadrate 18 Raunchy 19 Stoup 20 Toady
21 Umbles 22 Verbiage 23 Wallah 24 Zabaglione

6–8	Fair
9–11	Good
12–15	Very good
16–24	Excellent

FIFTY-SEVEN

1 Acrophobia 2 Baldwin 3 Chaucer 4 Dickens 5 Epiphany
6 Fitzgerald 7 Ginger 8 Haydn 9 Ibis 10 Jones
11 Kimono 12 Lauder 13 Metaphor 14 Numismatics
15 Orange 16 Phonetics 17 Quicklime 18 Ragamuffin
19 Snapdragon 20 Tyre 21 Urial 22 Vestry 23 Woodcock
24 Zombie

5–8	Fair
9–10	Good
11–14	Very good
15–24	Excellent

FIFTY-EIGHT

1 Anthrax 2 Bifurcate 3 Catamountain 4 Demerara
5 Epaulette 6 Febrile 7 Glengarry 8 Hepatitis 9 Innuendo
10 Jezebel 11 Kapok 12 Luddite 13 Myriad 14 Nice
15 Obelisk 16 Pandemonium 17 Quartering 18 Richter
19 Samlet 20 Tiffin 21 Udometer 22 Vasiform
23 Wildebeest 24 Xylem

5–8	Fair
9–10	Good
11–14	Very good
15–24	Excellent

FIFTY-NINE

1 Acronym 2 Bosworth 3 Comets 4 Danube 5 Enigma
6 Fife 7 Gibraltar 8 Horsa 9 Incandescent 10 Jenner
11 Kangaroo 12 Linseed 13 Montezuma 14 Nevis
15 Onion 16 Peary 17 Quebec 18 Reith 19 Sinhalese
20 Transjordan 21 Ululate 22 Vindicate 23 Walrus
24 Yang

5–8	Fair
9–10	Good
11–14	Very good
15–24	Excellent

SIXTY

1 Amontillado   2 Baksheesh   3 Cassata   4 Daiquiri
5 Euthanasia   6 Fido   7 Gamin   8 Hiatus   9 Iconoclast
10 Jeremiah   11 Koala   12 Leveret   13 Mezzanine
14 Nelson   15 Ocelot   16 Pachyderm   17 Quatorze
18 Rimose   19 Scission   20 Tawny   21 Urethra   22 Vegan
23 Wold   24 Xiphoid

5–8	Fair
9–10	Good
11–14	Very good
15–24	Excellent

SIXTY-ONE

1 Atlanta   2 Bauxite   3 Cocaine   4 Dauphin   5 Elucidate (or
Enlighten)   6 Ficus   7 Goldwyn   8 Hippocrates   9 Infallibility
10 Joshua   11 Kerosene   12 Litigation   13 Medina
14 Nemesis   15 Obsolescent   16 Pediment   17 Qwerty
18 Romanov   19 Sanskrit   20 Trees   21 Urals   22 Vintner
23 Worsted   24 Yawl

5–7	Fair
8–10	Good
11–14	Very good
15–24	Excellent

SIXTY-TWO

1 Ambergris   2 Beaujolais   3 Couloir   4 Dendrology
5 Encumbrance   6 Flageolet   7 Gossamer   8 Harlequin
9 Isthmus   10 Jackanapes   11 Kümmel   12 Lamella
13 Muu-muu   14 Negus   15 Oolong   16 Palindromes
17 Quadriga   18 Rhesus   19 Stanhope   20 Tepee
21 Upsilon   22 Viridescent   23 Wrack   24 Yaffle

5–7	Fair
8–10	Good
11–14	Very good
15–24	Excellent

SIXTY-THREE

1 Astaire 2 Bolivia 3 Checkers 4 Debussy 5 Escritoire
6 Fallacy 7 Glastonbury 8 Hydrophone 9 Ichthyology
10 Jettison 11 Kronborg 12 Lippizaner 13 Molière
14 Nepotism 15 Omnibuses 16 Pentateuch 17 Quinine
18 Rail 19 Salamander 20 Troglodyte 21 Uppsala
22 Virtuoso 23 Wallis 24 Yowl

5–7	Fair
8–10	Good
11–14	Very good
15–24	Excellent

SIXTY-FOUR

1 Apogee 2 Barathea 3 Crepuscular 4 Diablo 5 Emeritus
6 Filigree 7 Gotham 8 Hinny 9 Izzard 10 Jocose
11 Kursaal 12 Larrikin 13 Metalloid 14 Naiad
15 Ordnance 16 Paramour 17 Quadragenarian
18 Riparian 19 Spoor 20 Tarn 21 Upas 22 Valkyrie
23 Whimbrel 24 Zenana

5–7	Fair
8–10	Good
11–14	Very good
15–24	Excellent

SIXTY-FIVE

1 Armistice 2 Buchan 3 Copernicus 4 Delaware 5 Euchre
6 Faucet 7 Guadeloupe 8 Hood 9 Impugn 10 Jackal
11 Karma 12 Lutine 13 Mascagni 14 Nosegay 15 Oxides
16 Paisley 17 Quisling 18 Runyon 19 Softball 20 Tenter
21 Uranus 22 Vermont 23 Warhol 24 Yeats

5–7	Fair
8–10	Good
11–14	Very good
15–24	Excellent

SIXTY-SIX

1 Arroyo 2 Belladonna 3 Couleé 4 Deltoid 5 Ersatz
6 Farthingale 7 Gazebo 8 Hispid 9 Ilium 10 Jennet
11 Kittle 12 Lazar 13 Muffineer 14 Nigritude 15 Onager
16 Panoply 17 Quadraphonic 18 Recidivist 19 Stemma
20 Tangram 21 Urticate 22 Verglas 23 Wynd 24 Zilla

5–7	Fair
8–10	Good
11–14	Very good
15–24	Excellent

SIXTY-SEVEN

1 Apiarist 2 Brassica 3 Clowns 4 Dewar 5 Esau
6 Funchal 7 Gavotte 8 Horology 9 Imperialism 10 Jugular
11 Kariba 12 Lemur 13 Moriarty 14 Newgate
15 Orangemen 16 Pompey 17 Quadrennial 18 Rallying
19 Spiral 20 Torsion 21 Urdu 22 Vitreous 23 Whiting
24 Yonkers

5–7	Fair
8–10	Good
11–14	Very good
15–24	Excellent

SIXTY-EIGHT

1 Alfresco 2 Berserker 3 Clavate 4 Doge 5 Electrolier
6 Felaheen 7 Golem 8 Hirsute 9 Imago 10 Jasper
11 Kickshaw 12 Lascar 13 Monachal 14 Nodose
15 Oracle 16 Parabola 17 Quirt 18 Rhinal 19 Saggitate
20 Teg 21 Urceloate 22 Velar 23 Weasand 24 Zonda

5–7	Fair
8–10	Good
11–14	Very good
15–24	Excellent

SIXTY-NINE

1 Anthropology   2 Buddha   3 Coward   4 Dior   5 Elgar
6 Fujiyama   7 Gustavus   8 Hydrometer   9 Ionian   10 Jutland
11 Kinshasa   12 Lichen   13 Merckx   14 Nova   15 Octave
16 Pepys   17 Quince   18 Rial   19 Syntax   20 Turbot
21 Utrecht   22 Viola   23 Waterfalls   24 Zeno

5–7	Fair
8–10	Good
11–14	Very good
15–24	Excellent

SEVENTY

1 1 Arachnids   2 Bicephalous   3 Cachalot   4 Diurnal
5 Extrados   6 Fluvial   7 Gioconda   8 Huckaback   9 Ichthyoid
10 Janissary   11 Kerfuffle   12 Lysol   13 Macaque
14 Noisette   15 Olfactory   16 Panacea   17 Quotient
18 Rhizoid   19 Sapajou   20 Tandoor   21 Urbanite
22 Ventifact   23 Whare   24 Zymosis

5–7	Fair
8–10	Good
11–14	Very good
15–24	Excellent

SEVENTY-ONE

1 Aidan   2 Byzantium   3 Cesarewitch   4 Dogger   5 Euclid
6 Forum   7 Guinness   8 Harmonium   9 Ignoble   10 Jalopy
11 Kikuyu   12 Lacrosse   13 Manifest   14 November
15 Onomatopoeia   16 Polynesia   17 Quag   18 Rosetta
19 Shrubs   20 Tyburn   21 Uproarious   22 Variable
23 Whittle   24 Zaire

4–6	Fair
7–9	Good
10–13	Very good
14–24	Excellent

SEVENTY-TWO

1 Abigail   2 Behemoth   3 Cabana   4 Denizen (or Dweller)
5 Einkorn   6 Fizgig   7 Ginkgo   8 Haslet   9 Icterus
10 Jalousie   11 Korfball   12 Lutanist   13 Maremma
14 Nereid   15 Orcadian   16 Panga   17 Quilt   18 Riboflavin
19 Sulcus   20 Taurine   21 Ulginose   22 Vermian
23 Wampum   24 Yataghan

4–6	Fair
7–9	Good
10–13	Very good
14–24	Excellent

SEVENTY-THREE

1 Arnold   2 Bunyan   3 Cohan   4 Dragoon   5 Epstein
6 Firefly   7 Guillemot   8 Handy   9 Isotherm   10 Judaism
11 Keats   12 Liszt   13 Magnum   14 Naomi   15 Obelisk
16 Polonaise   17 Quietism   18 Rubicon   19 Sabre   20 Trent
21 Utrillo   22 Vagary   23 Wainscot   24 Zechariah

4–6	Fair
7–9	Good
10–13	Very good
14–24	Excellent

SEVENTY-FOUR

1 Alcade   2 Bonsai   3 Camelopard   4 Dorsal   5 Ectomorph
6 Fortissimo   7 Glossal   8 Homunculus   9 Imam   10 Jarrah
11 Kermes   12 Lanceolate   13 Marinade   14 Nuchal
15 Oread   16 Parkin   17 Quadruplicate   18 Reggae
19 Scutum   20 Ternary   21 Uhlan   22 Varicella
23 Woodchuck   24 Zygoma

4–6	Fair
7–9	Good
10–13	Very good
14–24	Excellent

SEVENTY-FIVE

1 Augustus 2 Barque 3 Carroll 4 Dylan 5 Everywhere
6 Forsythia 7 Gothic 8 Hertz 9 Iroquois 10 Julian
11 Kenya 12 Lithuania 13 Minuet 14 Nijinsky
15 Ormolu 16 Pharisee 17 Quaestor 18 Roach
19 Salchow 20 Tirana 21 Usurp 22 Valhalla 23 Weill
24 Ypres

4–6	Fair
7–9	Good
10–13	Very good
14–24	Excellent

SEVENTY-SIX

1 Alveolar 2 Bidonville 3 Cancroid 4 Doppelganger
5 Excrescent 6 Fleming 7 Gatling 8 Hamadryad 9 Intaglio
10 Jehu 11 Knag 12 Lambaste 13 Mahout 14 Noyade
15 Oedipus 16 Passerine 17 Quinquennial 18 Reclinate
19 Sapor 20 Tass 21 Usquebaugh 22 Violaceous
23 Withershins 24 Zein

4–6	Fair
7–9	Good
10–13	Very good
14–24	Excellent

SEVENTY-SEVEN

1 Appomattox 2 Bullion 3 Corsica 4 Decahedron
5 Eczema 6 Friedman 7 Gopher 8 Hindenburg 9 Idealism
10 Jacobites 11 Kinematics 12 Lutyens 13 Managua
14 Necromancer 15 Oligarchy 16 Ptolemy 17 Quatrain
18 Rockies 19 Solent 20 Timbuktu 21 Utensil
22 Vespucci 23 Wisconsin 24 Yalta

4–6	Fair
7–9	Good
10–13	Very good
14–24	Excellent

154

SEVENTY-EIGHT

1 Archipelago 2 Balalaika 3 Chignon 4 Dacha 5 Evulsion
6 Falciform 7 Gabion 8 Humdinger 9 Imbricate
10 Jacaranda 11 Kurd 12 Lactiferous 13 Marram
14 Nacarat 15 Obeah 16 Palmar 17 Quittance 18 Ragout
19 Swift 20 Tabloid 21 Unicorn 22 Verdigris 23 Warlock
24 Zeus

4–6	Fair
7–9	Good
10–13	Very good
14–24	Excellent

SEVENTY-NINE

1 Artichoke 2 Braddock 3 Cervantes 4 Dastard 5 Earhart
6 Florida 7 Golan 8 Heliotrope 9 Idiosyncrasy
10 Jungfrau 11 Kohlrabi 12 Latimer 13 Mandalay
14 Nictate 15 Odometer 16 Poseidon 17 Quezon 18 Roses
19 Showboat 20 Tiberius 21 Unadvised 22 Vanilla
23 Wallace 24 Ytterbium

4–6	Fair
7–9	Good
10–13	Very good
14–24	Excellent

EIGHTY

1 Argonauts 2 Bastinado 3 Chough 4 Decagon 5 Erst
6 Fieldfare 7 Gastropod 8 Hail 9 Illinois 10 Joplin
11 Kinkajou 12 Llama 13 Miasma 14 Nicotine 15 Oberon
16 Palmiped 17 Queens 18 Realtor 19 Shetland 20 Tabor
21 Underground 22 Vampire 23 Wrasse 24 Yale

4–6	Fair
7–9	Good
10–13	Very good
14–24	Excellent

EIGHTY-ONE

1 Allegory 2 Blériot 3 Chlorophyll 4 Dentist 5 Earwig
6 Fremantle 7 Goodman 8 Hygrometer 9 Iambus 10 Joule
11 Kalahari 12 Latvia 13 Marmoset 14 Nkrumah
15 Ounce 16 Pope 17 Quagga 18 Rushmore 19 Shelley
20 Trollope 21 Ulster 22 Vulgate 23 Windward
24 Xenophobia

4–5	Fair
6–8	Good
9–12	Very good
13–24	Excellent

EIGHTY-TWO

1 Amah 2 Bandicoot 3 Charivari 4 Demitasse 5 Ekka
6 Farruca 7 Gamba 8 Hunker 9 Ichor 10 Jerboa
11 Knob 12 Lacustrine 13 Muscadine 14 Nankeen
15 Occiput 16 Panjandrum 17 Quadratic 18 Rookery
19 Sirius 20 Toga 21 Umbriferous 22 Vespiary
23 Windsor 24 Ziegfeld

4–5	Fair
6–8	Good
9–12	Very good
13–24	Excellent

EIGHTY-THREE

1 Antwerp 2 Beet 3 Crustaceans 4 Dunlin 5 Eisenstein
6 Fillmore 7 Goebbels 8 Halley 9 Irving 10 Jeroboam
11 Karachi 12 Lisbon 13 Medici 14 Numbers 15 Orgies
16 Penniform 17 Qumran 18 Röntgen 19 Simile
20 Tolkein 21 Unction 22 Verde 23 Wilberforce
24 Yorktown

4–5	Fair
6–8	Good
9–12	Very good
13–24	Excellent

EIGHTY-FOUR

1 Axel   2 Basilisk   3 Calaboose   4 Dextral   5 Epergne
6 Filemot   7 Gasahol   8 Heliosis   9 Icosahedron   10 Jupiter
11 Khamsin   12 Latifundia   13 Minacious   14 Navarin
15 Odorous   16 Parados   17 Quintain   18 Rinderpest
19 Sciurine   20 Tenebrific   21 Uncouth   22 Voussoir
23 Wall-eyed   24 Zoril

4–5	Fair
6–8	Good
9–12	Very good
13–24	Excellent

EIGHTY-FIVE

1 Allenby   2 Boxing   3 Cuneiform   4 Dell   5 Ergonomics
6 Felucca   7 Goering   8 Holmes   9 Invar   10 Japonica
11 Kraal   12 Liffey   13 Museums   14 Nkomo   15 Osteopathy
16 Pharos   17 Quinquereme   18 Reynolds   19 Smooth
20 Tarsus   21 Umbra   22 Verne   23 Whatnot   24 Yukon

4–5	Fair
6–8	Good
9–12	Very good
13–24	Excellent

EIGHTY-SIX

1 Argot   2 Bacilliform   3 Caique   4 Dilettante   5 Exanimate
6 Flummery   7 Gazpacho   8 Hegira   9 Icitatus   10 Joyce
11 Knop   12 Lychnis   13 Melliferous   14 Nautch   15 Octad
16 Pavonine   17 Quiff   18 Ratskeller   19 Shabrack
20 Talipes   21 Unctuous   22 Vichyssoise   23 Warrigal
24 Zapata

4–5	Fair
6–8	Good
9–12	Very good
13–24	Excellent

EIGHTY-SEVEN

1 Angles 2 Bees 3 Cantabile 4 Darnley 5 Eurhythmics
6 Factotum 7 Gethsemane 8 Hydrology 9 Ikebana
10 Jerez 11 Kipling 12 Lepidopterist 13 Monkey
14 Nihilism 15 Obote 16 Plassey 17 Quadrille 18 Roget
19 Sumarian 20 Titicaca 21 Undulate 22 Visconti
23 Westminster 24 Zermatt

4–5	Fair
6–8	Good
9–11	Very good
12–24	Excellent

EIGHTY-EIGHT

1 Arboreal 2 Bayou 3 Calliope 4 Décolleté 5 Elocution
6 Fastigiate 7 Gasthaus 8 Hurricane 9 Indianapolis
10 Jacinth 11 Kabuki 12 Lachrymal 13 Mystagogue
14 Nephology 15 Obi 16 Palomino 17 Quatorzain
18 Reredos 19 Stroma 20 Tarboosh 21 Umber 22 Venose
23 Walk 24 Zanzibar

4–5	Fair
6–8	Good
9–11	Very good
12–24	Excellent

EIGHTY-NINE

1 Austen 2 Books 3 Cruziero 4 Dace 5 Entente 6 Faeroes
7 Googly 8 Hever 9 Isinglass 10 Jamb 11 Klapka
12 Louisiana 13 Mosel 14 Nicotiana 15 Oast 16 Phalanx
17 Quern 18 Richthofen 19 Shilling 20 Troposphere
21 Unequivocal 22 Vicissitude 23 Waterspout 24 Zephyr

4–5	Fair
6–8	Good
9–11	Very good
12–24	Excellent

NINETY

1 Anguine 2 Barbican 3 Cagoule 4 Dacoit 5 Exsanguinate
6 Fianchetto 7 Gambrel 8 Humoresque 9 Ichnography
10 Jardiniere 11 Kincob 12 Leporine 13 Melodeon
14 Neapolitan 15 Outfox 16 Palpate 17 Quadragesimal
18 Ramal 19 Sough 20 Terrazzo 21 Ultramarine
22 Vortiginous 23 Walpurgis 24 Yeoman

4–5	Fair
6–8	Good
9–11	Very good
12–24	Excellent

NINETY-ONE

1 Abelard 2 Bucephalus 3 Cochlea 4 Dunderhead
5 Emmet 6 Flanders 7 Gutenberg 8 Herbs 9 Inkerman
10 Jervis 11 Ketch 12 Lupine 13 Malapropism 14 Napier
15 Origami 16 Palk 17 Quadrumana 18 Ribbentrop
19 Smetana 20 Thane 21 Umbria 22 Verdigris
23 Warbeck 24 Zoophyte

3–4	Fair
5–7	Good
8–10	Very good
11–24	Excellent

NINETY-TWO

1 Aficionado 2 Baskerville 3 Cabochon 4 Down 5 Etna
6 Flight 7 Gingival 8 Hagiarchy 9 Ichneumon 10 Jesuits
11 Kingfisher 12 Lodestone 13 Mulatto 14 Namibia
15 Oleiferous 16 Pantheon 17 Quantum 18 Ratatouille
19 Sable 20 Thalamus 21 Umbles 22 Verger
23 Wolverine 24 Zucchetto

3–4	Fair
5–7	Good
8–10	Very good
11–24	Excellent

NINETY-THREE

1 Aramaic 2 Bering 3 Chlorine 4 Decameron 5 Eysenck
6 Flugelhorn 7 Gherkin 8 Hogshead 9 Irrawaddy
10 Joyce 11 Kedgeree 12 Libretto 13 Marat 14 Nehemiah
15 Orography 16 Punctuation 17 Quassia 18 Rabat
19 Speleologist 20 Thugs 21 Unciform 22 Vulpine
23 Wagner 24 Zloty

3–4	Fair
5–7	Good
8–10	Very good
11–24	Excellent

NINETY-FOUR

1 Abseil 2 Bawbee 3 Charm 4 Dross 5 Eddystone
6 Foliation 7 Ghurkas 8 Hircine 9 Insomnia 10 Jamaica
11 Kex 12 Lorcha 13 Myrobalan 14 Nijinsky
15 Obsequious 16 Paludal 17 Quetzal 18 Retrograde
19 Scorbutic 20 Tamarack 21 Ultima 22 Verwoerd
23 Woolsack 24 Zillion

3–4	Fair
5–7	Good
8–10	Very good
11–24	Excellent

NINETY-FIVE

1 Asunción 2 Bessemer 3 Catesby 4 Dulcinea
5 Etymology 6 Fetish 7 Golding 8 Honshu 9 Iceni
10 Jocasta 11 Kale 12 Lepanto 13 Macmillan
14 Nescience 15 Oppenheimer 16 Pendragon 17 Quincunx
18 Regicide 19 Sundials 20 Timbrel 21 Uhuru 22 Valois
23 Wapiti 24 Zoolite

3–4	Fair
5–7	Good
8–10	Very good
11–24	Excellent

NINETY-SIX

1 Acropolis 2 Babbitt 3 Calumet 4 Desert 5 Eldorado
6 Fresco 7 Ganja 8 Huckster 9 Imbrue 10 Jaeger
11 Kylix 12 Latakia 13 Mistral 14 Nereid 15 Oregon
16 Paradiddle 17 Quotidian 18 Ringhals 19 Switzerland
20 Taffy 21 Uxorious 22 Venezuela 23 Wankel 24 Yahoo

3–4	Fair
5–7	Good
8–10	Very good
11–24	Excellent

NINETY-SEVEN

1 Aboukir 2 Britannia 3 Colon 4 Drachma 5 Engels
6 Foch 7 Graves 8 Herodotus 9 Istria 10 Juxtaposed
11 Knowledge 12 Lumière 13 Marlow 14 Natatory
15 Oxymoron 16 Pinfold 17 Quintillion 18 Redeploy
19 Sinning 20 Toxicology 21 Ulm 22 Vargas 23 Wisteria
24 Zareba

3–4	Fair
5–7	Good
8–9	Very good
10–24	Excellent

NINETY-EIGHT

1 Arcturus 2 Basinet 3 Chattering 4 Duodenum
5 Escoffier 6 Fritillaries 7 Gopher 8 Hippogriff 9 Interstice
10 Jocose 11 Kibble 12 Lithium 13 Moa 14 Neolithic
15 Opthalmic 16 Palfrey 17 Quonset 18 Richesse 19 Sofia
20 Tactile 21 Urning 22 Victoria 23 Wedlock 24 Zener

3–4	Fair
5–7	Good
8–9	Very good
10–24	Excellent

NINETY-NINE

1 Arno   2 Bonneville   3 Catenary   4 Dipthong
5 Entomology   6 Fisher   7 Gujarat   8 Hartebeest
9 Ichnology   10 Jenkins   11 Krill   12 Lohengrin
13 Metonymy   14 Negrillos   15 Okapi   16 Phycology
17 Quetzal   18 Rebus   19 Shantung   20 Torture
21 Ullswater   22 Vanuatu   23 Wakefield   24 Xylography

3–4	Fair
5–7	Good
8–9	Very good
10–24	Excellent

1 Angelus   2 Bodega   3 Clowder   4 Dopping   5 Esculent
6 Fibonacci   7 Greengage   8 Harvestman   9 Inquiline
10 Jellyfish   11 Kymograph   12 Lectern   13 Mongolia
14 Nihility   15 Obfuscate   16 Palmetto   17 Quasar
18 Reddle   19 Strigose   20 Taipan   21 Uraeus   22 Vagary
23 Wyvern   24 Zebu

3–4	Fair
5–7	Good
8–9	Very good
10–24	Excellent

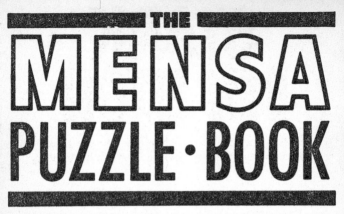

THE MENSA PUZZLE · BOOK

PHILIP CARTER & KEN RUSSELL

This challenging collection of Mensa puzzles is not for the faint-hearted. You'll need all your wits about you to solve the dazzling range of brainteasers – crosswords, word and number games, grid and diagram puzzles – a veritable cornucopia of craftiness.

THE ULTIMATE QUIZ BOOK FOR THE ULTIMATE QUIZ ADDICT

0 7474 0018 7   CROSSWORDS/QUIZZES   £2.99

STARK
BEN ELTON

Stark have more money than God and the social
conscience of a dog on a croquet lawn. What's more,
they know the Earth is dying.

Deep in Western Australia where the Aboriginals used
to milk the trees, a planet-sized plot takes shape. Some
green freaks pick up the scent. A Pommie poseur, a
brain-fried Vietnam Vet, Aboriginals who lost their land
. . . not much against a conspiracy that controls society.
But EcoAction isn't in society; it just lives in the same
place, along with the cockroaches.

If you're facing the richest and most disgusting
conspiracy in history, you have to do more than stick up
two fingers and say "peace".

0 7474 40390 2   GENERAL FICTION

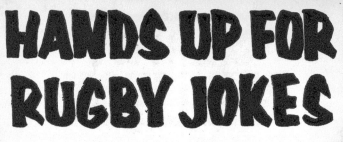

HANDS UP FOR
RUGBY JOKES

THEY STUCK 'EM UP . . .

Their hands that is, when we asked who wanted yet another
collection of the fastest-selling, hilarious, most bawdy load of laughs
ever to grace the greasy floor of your rugby club locker room. They
demanded, cajoled, bribed and bothered us until we came up with
the goods!!

So here it is, pull your pinkies from your pint and let's have a hand
for Bill and his Bong, Walker the great talker, the young gasman
from Chester who had terrible wind, the Morris Dancer and the
Yorkshire minor . . . and many many more!!

And don't forget to intercept:
RUGBY JOKES
SON OF RUGBY JOKES
MORE RUGBY JOKES
WHAT RUGBY JOKES DID NEXT
EVEN MORE RUGBY JOKES
RUGBY JOKES SCORE AGAIN
RUGBY SONGS
MORE RUGBY SONGS
RUGBY JOKES IN THE OFFICE
Also available in Sphere Books

0 7221 7256 7   HUMOUR

MARLON BRANDO

David Shipman

He has been called *the* American actor; a blindingly intelligent man who invented 'method' acting and revolutionised his craft. He has also been accused of despising acting; 'mumbling', 'scratching' and 'itching' his way through films. While Elia Kazan thought he was a genius, Trevor Howard claimed that he had never met an actor who took so little pride in his work.

Marlon Brando rose to international fame in *A Streetcar Named Desire*, broke box-office records in *On the Waterfront*, rescued a flagging career in *The Godfather*, and scandalised the world with *Last Tango in Paris*. Yet he still remains an enigma – a Hollywood legend who refused to play the Hollywood game.

David Shipman traces Brando's career to the present day, providing new insights into the complex character who has provoked more anger and admiration than any actor of his generation. And he also follows Brando's extraordinary private life; a life marked by scandals involving children, wives and ex-wives – and his historic refusal to accept an Oscar for his most memorable role.

'Brilliant . . . a very straight-ahead account of the Great Adenoid. Shipman's great virtue is that he never goes soft on you; judgement and information come first and second, and adulation last'
Russell Davies, Observer

0 7474 0431 3   BIOGRAPHY

All Sphere Books are available at your bookshop or newsagent, or can be ordered from the following address: Sphere Books, Cash Sales Department, P.O. Box 11, Falmouth, Cornwall TR10 9EN

Please send cheque or postal order (no currency), and allow 60p for postage and packing for the first book plus 25p for the second book and 15p for each additional book ordered up to a maximum charge of £1.90 in U.K.

B.F.P.O. customers allow 60p for the first book, 25p for the second book plus 15p per copy for the next 7 books thereafter 9p per book.

Overseas customers, including Eire, please allow £1.25 for postage and packing for the first book, 75p for the second book and 28p for each subsequent title ordered.

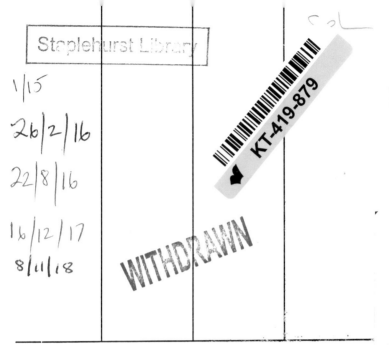

WITHDRAWN

KT-419-879

Books should be returned or renewed by the last date above. Renew by phone **08458 247 200** or online *www.kent.gov.uk/libs*

Libraries & Archives

CUSTOMER SERVICE EXCELLENCE

The Government Standard

UK

For Anna – welcome to the world! ~ A M

For Rachel and Emma ~ D R

STRIPES PUBLISHING
An imprint of Little Tiger Press
1 The Coda Centre, 189 Munster Road,
London SW6 6AW

A paperback original
First published in Great Britain in 2015

Text copyright © Alan MacDonald, 2015
Illustrations copyright © David Roberts, 2015

ISBN: 978-1-84715-462-0

Printed and bound in the UK.

10 9 8 7 6 5 4 3 2 1

Angela Nicely

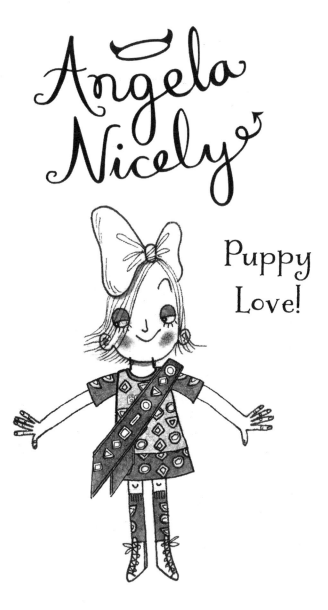

Puppy Love!

ALAN MACDONALD ILLUSTRATED BY DAVID ROBERTS

stripes

Have you read the other *Angela Nicely* books?

Contents

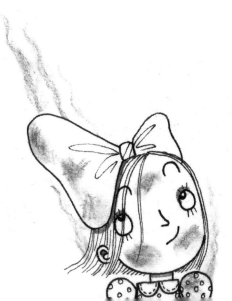

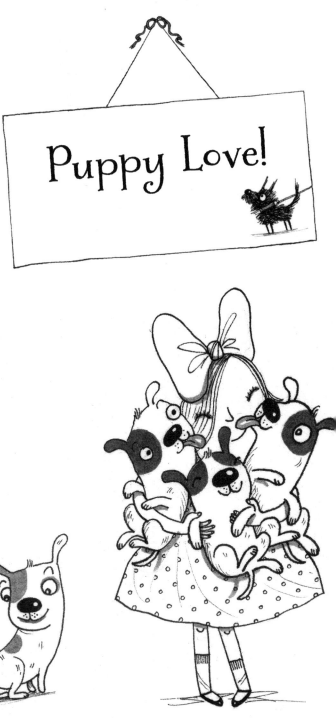

Puppy Love!

Chapter 1

Angela sploshed milk on to her cereal and looked up.

"I saw a puppy yesterday," she announced.

"Mmm?" said Mrs Nicely, closing the dishwasher.

"A little brown and white puppy. It was sitting outside the chip shop,"

Angela went on.

"Really," said Mrs Nicely.

"I think it was lost," Angela said hopefully.

Mrs Nicely gave Angela one of her looks. She knew where this conversation was going. "It wasn't lost, Angela," she sighed. "The owner was probably in the shop and they'd left the dog outside."

"But what if it's still there?" asked Angela. "What if it's all alone with no one to look after it?"

Mrs Nicely rolled her eyes. "Angela, how many times? We are not getting a dog!" she said.

Angela tilted her head to one side. "Just a teeny-weeny puppy?" she pleaded.

"NO!" groaned her mum. "Dogs are

8

smelly and dirty and way too much trouble."

"Not if you train them," argued Angela.

"And what about the mess?" demanded Mrs Nicely. "Who's going to clear up when it does its … business … on my lawn?"

"Me!" said Angela. "And I would take it to the park for a walk *every* day. Please, Mum, you'd LOVE a puppy once you got used to it."

"You know I hate dogs," said Mrs Nicely. "And besides, we've just got a new sofa. I don't want it covered in dog hair, thank you very much."

Angela pulled a face. Who cared about a sofa? She'd been begging her meanie parents to buy her a puppy for months, but the answer was always the same. N-O spells NO. Maybe she could give her dad another try?

Angela went out into the garden to find him. "Da-ad, wouldn't *you* like a puppy?" she asked.

Her dad laughed. "What did your mum say?" he asked.

Angela pulled a face.

"She said 'no'."

"Then there's no point talking about it," said Dad. "In any case, we've got a cat."

"It's not the same," grumbled Angela. "You can't teach Pusskins tricks or take him for a walk."

"Well, we can't have both," said Dad. "Dogs and cats don't mix."

"Some do," argued Angela. "And my puppy would be so sweet."

"Hmm, try telling your mother that," said Mr Nicely. "She doesn't want a dog and nothing's ever going to change that."

Angela hung her head. It wasn't fair. Bertie next door had a dog called Whiffer and Dora in her class had the cutest puppy in the world. Why was she the only one who wasn't allowed a dog? Angela thought she'd be good with dogs. She would take the puppy for walks, and teach it to sit up and roll over – though probably not on the new sofa.

There had to be some way to convince her mum! Angela had asked for a puppy for Christmas. She'd left pictures of sad-eyed puppies around the house. She'd even written PUPPY in big letters on her mum's shopping list. But nothing had had any effect. All the same, Angela wasn't giving up yet. She went back inside.

"Mu-um," she said. "What if the puppy—"

"NO, ANGELA!" shouted Mrs Nicely. "And if you ask me again I will scream!"

Chapter 2

Later that morning, Angela went to the park with her friends. They sat on the roundabout.

"It's not fair!" complained Angela. "I've tried everything but they just say 'no'."

"You just have to keep on and on till they give in," said Maisie. "That's what I do when I want something."

"I've tried that," sighed Angela. "I've asked, like, a million times!"

Laura set the roundabout moving and clung on. "There ought to be a dog library," she said.

Angela looked puzzled. "Dogs can't read," she said.

"No, I mean a library for borrowing a dog," Laura explained. "You know, like getting a book out."

"Yes," laughed Maisie. "Then when you got tired of it, you could take it back."

It wasn't a bad idea, thought Angela. Imagine a library with hundreds of dogs sitting on the shelves! You could try a different dog each week to see which one you liked most. She sighed heavily. If only a dog library actually existed!

But maybe there were other ways…

If she could prove to her parents that she could look after a dog, maybe they'd give in? Who would lend her one? Not Bertie, for a start. Besides, her mum complained about Whiffer all the time. Angela looked around – the park was full of dogs. Hairy dogs, yappy dogs, small dogs, spotty dogs – all out for a walk with their owners. Angela's eyes lit up. She had the answer!

"DOG WALKING!" she cried, jumping off the roundabout. "I could walk them for other people."

Maisie frowned. "Who's going to let you walk their dog?" she asked.

"Hundreds of people," said Angela. "Come on, all we need is a poster."

Angela found a big piece of card in a bin and Laura lent her a pen. Five minutes later she had made a large sign.

DOG TiRed?
try Angela's dog
Walking Servis
FREE
ASK Tooday

Maisie shook her head. "Come on, Angela!" she said. "You don't think anyone's going to trust you with their dog?"

"Why not?" said Angela. "I'm only borrowing them. I bet if I stand here long enough I'll get tons of customers."

She stood by the path holding her sign. A few dog owners passed by and smiled at her, but none of them stopped. Angela held the sign higher above her head in case people couldn't read it. The next person to come by was a boy from their class at school. Ryan had a big red dog called Max.

"What's all this?" he asked, stopping.

"Angela's Dog Walking Service," explained Angela. "I could walk Max if you like."

"I'm walking him already," Ryan pointed out.

"Yes, but if I did it, then you could go and buy an ice cream," suggested Angela.

Ryan hadn't thought of that. Dog walking was hard work and he quite fancied an ice cream.

DOG Tired?
try Angela's dog
Walking Servis
FREE
Ask Tooday

"What's the catch?" he asked.

"There isn't a catch," said Laura.

"Angela just loves dogs," explained Maisie. "And she needs one to practise on."

Ryan scratched his arm, thinking it over. "I'll need him back in an hour," he said.

"No problem," said Angela. That would give her enough time to get Max home and show him off.

"And don't let him roll in the mud – he loves mud," warned Ryan.

Angela nodded, taking hold of Max's lead. This was easy! She didn't know why she'd never thought of dog walking before.

Chapter 3

Angela and her friends walked Max once round the park, heading for the gates. On their way they passed an old lady sitting on a bench. Mrs Crab lived over the road from Angela with her little terrier, Scruff.

"Hi, Mrs Crab!" cried Angela. "Are you taking Scruff for a walk?"

"I am, dear," said Mrs Crab. "But I've just stopped for a breather."

"We could walk him for you," offered Angela. "We're doing dog walking today!"

"Are you? What a good idea!" smiled Mrs Crab. "I'd be ever so grateful. Scruff likes to run but these days I can't keep up with him."

"We'll see you in an hour," said Angela. This was brilliant. This morning she didn't have any dogs and now she had TWO! Her parents were going to be so impressed when they saw her looking after them.

Max and Scruff were soon getting to know each other, which involved a lot of bottom-sniffing. Max was twice Angela's size and dragged her along like a shopping

trolley. Laura, meanwhile, was meant to be in charge of Scruff, but the little dog kept zooming off in all directions.

"Not that way!" cried Angela.

"I'm trying!" groaned Laura, tugging at the lead. "He won't listen to me!"

The two dogs began to chase each other in circles, barking excitedly. Soon their leads were tangled round Angela's legs till she looked like a parcel tied with string.

Maisie giggled. "I thought you were supposed to be walking them, not playing games!"

"Well, don't just stand there, help me!" cried Angela.

They finally managed to untangle the dog leads. But just as they were heading out of the park, Max caught sight of something … a sandpit!

Sand! Dirt! Digging! WOOF! He bolted away, with Scruff chasing after him. Angela was dragged along at supersonic speed until she tripped and landed face down in a flowerbed. When she looked up, the two dogs were digging madly, with sand flying in all directions.

She hurried over to fetch them. "Are these dogs yours?" demanded a woman, clutching her toddler.

"No … er, well … yes," said Angela.

"Then you should keep them under control," snapped the woman. "Can't you read?" She pointed to a big notice on the fence, which said "NO DOGS ALLOWED!".

Angela turned red and pulled Max and Scruff away.

"This is going well," grinned Maisie. "I thought you said that dog walking was easy."

Angela sighed. "Let's just get them back to my house before anything else happens," she said.

Laura eyed the two filthy dogs. "Are you sure your mum and dad won't mind?" she asked.

"Of course not," said Angela. "The whole point is to show them I can look after dogs."

They managed to drag the dogs along Angela's road without any further disasters. Scruff insisted on sniffing every lamppost while Max tried to nose in the dustbins.

Outside her house, Angela stopped.
"Now remember, they've got to sit still
and behave," she told Maisie and Laura.
"They mustn't bark or run around."

"Try telling them that!" laughed
Maisie.

Laura didn't see how she was meant
to get Scruff to sit. He couldn't keep
still for two seconds!
Although right now
he was sitting on the
driveway. *Uh-oh*,
she thought, *he
isn't just sitting…*

Chapter 4

The girls stared in horror as Scruff
wagged his tail, pleased with himself.

"EWW! That stinks!" said Maisie,
holding her nose.

"It's only dog poo," said Angela with
a sigh.

"But who's going to clear it up?"
asked Laura.

The girls all took a step backwards.

"Don't look at me," said Laura.

"Well, I'm not touching it," said Maisie. "This was *your* idea, Angela."

Angela looked down at the smelly do-do on the driveway. Her mum would go up the wall if she saw it. But how could they remove it without a pooper scoop? When she got her own puppy Angela was going to have a pooper scoop with an extra-long handle. In the meantime, they would just have to leave Scruff's mess until she could find a spade or something. The important thing was to get the dogs into the house unseen. Wouldn't her mum get a surprise when she found two dogs sitting obediently in the kitchen?

Angela opened the side gate and

beckoned to the others to follow. She could see her mum in the garden, digging.

"IS THAT YOU, ANGELA?" called Mrs Nicely without looking round.

"I'm with Maisie and Laura!" shouted Angela. "We're just getting a drink!"

They led the dogs down the side passage and in through the back door. Scruff went padding around the kitchen. Max sniffed the air, smelling something.

"Now, what shall we feed them?" asked Angela.

"Dog food," replied Laura.

"We don't have any, only cat food!" said Angela.

Her mouth fell open. *Cat food?* She'd forgotten all about Pusskins! She hoped he was sleeping on a bed upstairs…

RUFF!

Angela spotted Pusskins in the hall at the same time as Max. The cat arched his back and hissed.

"MAX, NO! STAY!" ordered Angela, in her firmest voice.

It was no use. The dogs zoomed past her as Pusskins shot out of sight. For a podgy moggy he could move surprisingly fast. Angela dashed into the hall.

NOOOOO! The dogs were in the lounge!

Pusskins had climbed on top of the shelves and was yowling at the dogs. Max and Scruff stood on the sofa, barking excitedly.

HISSSS!

WOOF! WOOF!

The noise brought Mrs Nicely running in from the garden. Her hands flew to her face as she let out a scream.

"EEEEK! MY NEW SOFA!"

Angela had forgotten about the new sofa. It was covered in sandy brown pawprints and one of the cushions looked a bit torn.

Mrs Nicely's face was purple with rage. She turned to Angela.

"Who let these filthy dogs in the house?" she yelled. "Angela, is this your doing?"

Angela gulped. "It wasn't my fault. We were looking after them," she said.

"Well, you can take them back to where they came from, right now!" thundered her mum.

Angela nodded sadly. With her friends' help, she managed to drag Max and Scruff out of the door. Mrs Nicely marched down the drive after them.

"And you can pay for the damage out of your— UGH!"

She broke off and looked down. She'd trodden in something horrid. It looked like…

"ANGELAAAAAAAAAAAAAAAA!" howled Mrs Nicely.

Angela didn't look back. She guessed she wouldn't be getting a puppy after all. Not this week, anyway.

Chapter 1

SLOP! SPLAT! SPLODGE! Angela's
class were busy painting. Miss Darling
wanted them to make a summer display
to brighten up the entrance hall. Angela
splodged more paint on to her picture
of a mermaid riding a dolphin. Suddenly
she bent down and stared at the
newspaper which was covering the floor.

"Hey look at this, Laura," she whispered, pointing.

Teacher of the Year!

This year's winner will be announced next week.
Last year's winner, Miss Spooner, is pictured with her trophy.

Angela's eyes lit up. "Teacher of the Year!" she said.

"Well, what about it?" asked Laura.

Angela looked at her. "Can't you think of someone we know who should be Teacher of the Year?" she asked.

Laura frowned. "Mr Weakly?" she suggested.

"Are you barmy bonkers?" said Angela. "I mean Miss Darling!"

"Ohhh, Miss Darling," said Laura, nodding. "Yes, she'd be perfect. Has she entered then?"

"I doubt it," said Angela. "But someone ought to vote for her."

Maisie wandered over to join them, dripping paint on the floor. Angela showed her the article.

"Angela thinks Miss Darling ought to be Teacher of the Year," explained Laura.

"Definitely," agreed Maisie. "She's the best teacher in the school – probably in the whole world."

"Do we get a vote?" asked Laura.

"Course not," said Maisie. "No one asks what children think."

"Then who decides?" asked Laura.

It was a good question and for once

Angela was stuck for an answer. All she knew was that Miss Darling was the best class teacher she had ever had. She was kind and patient and listened to everyone – even Tiffany Charmers, who put her hand up fifty times a day.

"I know," said Angela. "We could make a list."

"What sort of list?" asked Laura.

"A list of reasons why Miss Darling ought to win," said Angela. She wrote the list in splodgy yellow paint.

1. DUSNT SHOUT
2. HARDLY NEVER GETS CROSS
3. WARES NICE EARINGS.
4. ALWAYS USULLY LETS US TALK IN KLASS.

Angela was about to add one more reason, when she noticed Miss Darling standing over them.

"What's all this?" the teacher asked.

Angela turned bright pink. "Nothing!" she said. "We were just, um…"

"…just talking about Tiffany," said Maisie quickly.

"Well, you're meant to be getting on with your painting," frowned Miss Darling. "More work and less chatter, please."

They waited until she had gone, then Angela quickly painted over the list. "That was close. She mustn't find out," she said.

"Why not?" asked Laura.

"Because it's got to be a surprise when she wins," said Angela.

Miss Darling was going to be so thrilled when she heard the news. Imagine it, Teacher of the Year! There would be a picture in the paper with Miss Darling and Angela holding the trophy. But there was just one small problem – how to make sure Miss Darling won?

Chapter 2

Angela decided to ask her dad's advice after school. She found him upstairs at the computer.

"Dad?" she said. "You know teachers?"

"Mmm-hmm," said Dad.

"Well, how do they win stuff like rewards?" asked Angela.

Dad looked puzzled. "Rewards?"

Angela Nicely

"Yes, you know, like Teacher of the Year rewards," said Angela.

"Ah, I think you mean awards," said Dad. "I didn't know there was a Teacher of the Year."

"It was in the newspaper!" said Angela. "But how do you win?"

Her dad laughed. "I don't know, I'm not a teacher," he said.

"I know *that*," sighed Angela. "It's Miss Darling we want to win."

"Oh, I see," said Dad. "Well, I guess she'd have to do something special, besides trying to teach you lot."

Angela frowned. "Special?"

"Yes, to get her noticed, like – I don't know – saving a child from drowning."

Angela considered this. They went swimming every other Friday, but so

far no one had come near drowning.
Anyway, Miss Darling stayed on the
side and didn't even get her feet wet.
If she was going to win Teacher of the
Year she'd have to try a lot harder.

The next day at school Angela called
a meeting of the GOBS club (GIRLS
ONLY, BOYS SMELL).

As usual Angela opened the meeting.

"Well, I asked my dad," she said. "And
he says you've just got to get noticed."

"Who has?" asked Laura, confused.

"Miss Darling of course, if she wants to
be Teacher of the Year," replied Angela.

"We don't even know if she wants to,"
Maisie pointed out. "She might not."

Angela gave her a weary look.

"Of course she wants to, Maisie," she said. "But it's no good her just marking books and stuff, she has to do something amazing."

They sat in silence for a while, trying to think.

"She could dye her hair pink," said Maisie. "My cousin Kylie did that and everyone noticed."

Angela shook her head. She didn't think pink hair would help to win Teacher of the Year.

"What if she became famous?" asked Laura. "Maybe she could be the first teacher in space!"

"That would get you noticed!" said Angela. But she doubted Miss Darling had time to train as an astronaut on top of teaching her class.

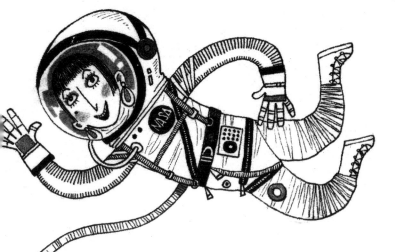

"My dad says she could save someone or something," explained Angela.

"She could save Tiffany from being eaten by a crocodile!" suggested Laura.

"I wouldn't save her," said Maisie. "And where are we going to find a crocodile?"

"Well, maybe not a crocodile," said Angela. "But I know where to find a tiger."

The other two looked at her in surprise. "Where?" they asked.

"In my room," said Angela. "I got a tiger onesie for Christmas."

"Don't be stupid," said Maisie. "You can't save someone from a tiger onesie!"

"You haven't seen it," replied Angela. "It's got eyes and ears and everything. I bet if you wore it, people would think it was a real tiger."

Laura looked doubtful. "But who's going to come to school dressed as a tiger?" she asked.

Uh-oh. Angela and Maisie were both looking at her with funny expressions.

"No way!" she said.

Chapter 3

The next day, Angela brought her
tiger onesie into school, hidden in her
backpack. She took it out to show her
friends when no one was around. It had
two green eyes, striped fur and a long tail.

"Cool!" said Maisie. "That looks
brilliant!"

Laura didn't seem convinced. "I'm

not wearing that. I'll look stupid," she
grumbled.

"No, you won't," said Angela.
"Anyway, if it's zipped up, no one will
see your face."

"Except Miss Darling," said Maisie.

"Not even her," said Angela. "You
can hide in the toilets and we'll tell her
there's an escaped tiger."

"But how will anyone know I'm a
tiger if I'm hiding?" asked Laura.

"They'll probably look in through the
door for a second," said Angela. "But
you can growl like a tiger about to eat
them and they're bound to soon run out
before they realize it's you. Go on, try it."

Laura sighed and took a breath.
"Grrr," she said.

"Not like that!" groaned Angela.

"You're meant to scare people to death!"

Laura screwed up her face and tried again. "GRRRRRRRR!"

"You sound like my gran when she's eaten too much," said Maisie. "You're going to have to practise."

Angela's plan was for the three of them to slip into the girls' toilets at break time. As soon as Laura changed into her costume, Angela and Maisie would raise the alarm. Once Miss Darling caught a glimpse of the tiger she would stay outside the door. At that point, Laura could quickly get changed and they'd say that the tiger had escaped through a window, all thanks to Miss Darling. It was a good plan – at least, Angela thought so.

Chapter 4

DRRRINNG!

The bell rang for break time. Angela and her friends hurried out and slipped into the girls' toilets. Laura got changed into the tiger costume while Maisie guarded the main door.

"Remember," said Angela. "Stay on all fours and make lots of noise."

Laura zipped up the tiger suit.

"But what if someone comes?" she worried.

"They won't," said Angela.

"And if they do, growl at them. GRRRR!" said Maisie.

Laura sighed. Maisie was much better at growling. Why couldn't *she* dress up as the tiger?

"Wait until Miss Darling has got a look at you, then get changed," said Angela. "We'll say she scared the tiger away."

Laura pulled down the hood and zipped it up tight. Why, oh why, had she let Angela talk her into this? She got down on all fours, trying to look like a fierce tiger.

"Let's go," said Angela, giving Laura a thumbs up.

WHAM! Angela and Maisie burst out of the toilets, almost bumping into Tiffany Charmers outside.

"HEEEEELP! A TIGER!" screamed Angela.

"What?" said Tiffany, covering her ears.

"A TIGER! IN THE TOILETS! Don't go in there!" cried Maisie.

"Oh, HA HA, very funny," said Tiffany sarcastically. She pushed open the door…

"GRRRRR!"

Tiffany quickly slammed the door shut and stood against it, turning pale.

"There's a … a … TIGER!" she stammered. "I saw its back!"

Angela nodded. "I know! We tried to tell you!"

"Well, what are we waiting for?" asked Tiffany. "We've got to find a teacher!"

Out in the playground Miss Darling was chatting to a group of infants.

Suddenly she was interrupted by loud shrieks as three girls burst out of the school.

"THERE'S A TIGER!" squealed Tiffany.

"In the toilets!" gasped Maisie.

"It almost gobbled us up!" added Angela, for dramatic effect.

Miss Darling took a deep breath. "Okay, calm down," she said. "Now tell me slowly, what's the matter?"

"A TIGER!" panted Angela. "It's got into the girls' toilets. You've got to come now!"

Miss Darling raised her eyes to the heavens.

"A tiger?" she said. "Is this some kind of game, Angela?"

57

"No, Miss, it's true, honestly!" said Angela.

"Maybe I should take a look," smiled Miss Darling.

Angela couldn't see what there was to smile about – this was a matter of life and death! And she wished Miss Darling would hurry up because a crowd was starting to gather. Suddenly Miss Boot appeared, stomping across the playground towards them.

"WHAT'S GOING ON?" she boomed.

Miss Darling raised her eyebrows again. "The girls think they've seen a tiger," she said.

"A tiger? Don't be ridiculous! Where?" demanded Miss Boot.

"In the girls' toilets!" answered Angela.

58

"If this is your idea of a joke, Angela…" said Miss Boot.

"It isn't, Miss," said Angela. "We saw it!"

"Very well, show me," said Miss Boot.

They all set off with Angela leading the way. Angela felt things weren't going exactly to plan. Miss Darling was meant to save the school, not Miss Boot.

A minute later, they were standing outside the girls' toilets. Miss Boot banged on the door, armed with a mop from the caretaker's cupboard.

"Who's in there? Answer me!" she barked.

They waited a few seconds.

"GRRRrrrRRrr!" The tiger didn't sound too sure of itself.

"See? A tiger," said Angela. "But maybe if we don't bother him, he'll go away."

Miss Boot shook her head. "If that's a tiger, I'm a monkey's aunt," she said, banging on the door again. "COME OUT! DO YOU HEAR ME?"

"GRRrrrr," went the tiger, a note of panic creeping into its voice.

"That's it," snorted Miss Boot. "I'm going in!"

WHAM!

Miss Boot burst into the toilets waving her mop in one hand. The tiger screamed and scuttled away, but Miss Boot grabbed it by the tail.

"ARGHHH!" squawked the tiger as it was dragged across the floor.

"LAURA?" said Miss Darling. "Is that you?"

Laura sat up and pulled down her hood to reveal her face.

"It was Angela's idea," she sniffed. "She MADE me do it!"

Uh-oh, thought Angela, now there was going to be trouble.

"We were only trying to help!" she said.

"Help? Help who?" asked Miss Boot.

62

"Miss Darling," said Angela. "We wanted her to win Teacher of the Year. We thought if she rescued us from a tiger it would help!"

Miss Darling looked stern, though she was trying not to laugh. "ANGELA!" she groaned.

But Miss Boot did not see the funny side. Pretending to be a tiger was against the rules and the Head would have to be told.

The next morning at breakfast Angela's dad was reading the newspaper. Suddenly he cried out, "Oh look, Teacher of the Year!"

"What? Where?" said Angela.

Her dad read out the article.

TEACHER OF THE YEAR
IS BLOOMING MARVELLOUS

Betty Dripworthy was yesterday
named Teacher of the Year. Miss
Dripworthy and her class have
turned their unloved schoolyard
into a flower garden.

"You've got to be kidding!" groaned
Angela. After all the trouble they'd
gone to for Miss Darling's sake, the
winner had simply planted a bunch of
flowers! Really, thought Angela, there
was no justice in the world.

Chapter 1

Angela leaped out of bed. Yabadoozy!
It was Friday – the day she was going
to Brownie camp. A whole weekend
camping with her friends! Sleeping in
a tent, making campfires and having
midnight feasts every night. It was
going to be the greatest trip ever!

Angela had never been camping before.

Her mum couldn't see the point.
Why sleep on a lumpy airbed in the
freezing cold, she said, when you could
be tucked up in your own bed? But
Angela thought that camping would
be a great adventure. Her best friends
Maisie and Laura were going, and
Tiffany Charmers, too – worse luck.

Tiffany had joined
Brownies a month
before Angela,
which meant
that she was the
world expert.
She already
had a sash full of
badges, which she
showed Angela
every week.

So far Angela only had two badges – Road Safety and the Brownie badge, which didn't really count. Still, Brown Owl said that they could earn new badges at camp. Angela couldn't wait. She was going to collect so many badges that she would need a bigger uniform to make room for them all.

At five o' clock, Angela's mum walked her to the church hall. Maisie and Laura were there, loading their bags into the minibus.

Soon they were heading out of town and into the countryside. Brown Owl and Tawny Owl sat in the front seat.

"So, who's been camping before?" asked Brown Owl, turning round.

"I have," said Laura. "In the back garden."

"Huh! That's not REAL camping," scoffed Tiffany. "I've stayed on a campsite dozens of times."

"Really?" said Brown Owl. "And where do you go camping, Tiffany?"

"In France, every summer," boasted

70

Tiffany. "It's the best campsite in the universe! It's got a restaurant, a playground and three swimming pools!"

"Hmm," said Brown Owl. "Well, you might find this weekend a little different."

As the sun sank, the bus turned down a bumpy track and finally came to a halt. The girls piled out, eager to look around. The campsite was in a scrubby field, surrounded by trees. There was a barn, a cow field next door and little else.

"Where are the tents?" asked Tiffany.

"We've brought our own," replied Brown Owl, unloading the bags.

"But I can't see a swimming pool!" grumbled Tiffany.

"No!" laughed Brown Owl. "If you want a swim there's a river right there."

Tiffany looked horrified. She wasn't swimming in a freezing cold river. There might be frogs, or other slimy creatures.

Laura was looking around anxiously. "Where's the bathroom?" she asked.

"Over there," said Tawny Owl, pointing to the rickety old barn. "There's a cold tap, a sink and a toilet next door. Everything we need."

Tiffany held her head. "We've got to wash in a BARN? In COLD WATER?" she wailed.

"It won't kill you," grinned Brown Owl.

"UGHHH!" yelled Tiffany, stomping off in a sulk.

Angela thought Tiffany might have

gone home there and then if she could.
No baths or hot showers – by the end
of the weekend they were going to be
so dirty!

Chapter 2

Brown Owl divided them into six groups and gave each one a tent. Angela was sharing with Maisie and Laura, while Alice and Suki were stuck with Tiffany. None of them had ever put up a tent before, so Brown Owl showed them how to do it. Angela thought it didn't look that difficult.

After several attempts and a lot of arguments, Angela's group finally got the tent to stay up. As it grew dark, everyone sat round the campfire, eating sausages and beans. Then Brown Owl packed them all off to bed.

"I shall be coming round at nine in the morning for tent inspection," she warned. "And I expect every tent to be neat and tidy. The group with the tidiest tent over the weekend will earn their Camper badges."

Camper badges? Angela's eyes lit up. She needed that badge badly. For a start, it was one badge that smartypants Tiffany didn't have. She would turn green with envy every time she set eyes on it. All Angela had to do was keep the tent perfectly tidy – what could be simpler?

75

Later that night, Angela and her friends lay in their sleeping bags. Clothes and boots were scattered around the tent. Their plan was to get up early to tidy the tent before inspection.

Laura sat up. "ANGELA!" she hissed. "Are you awake?"

"Mmm," mumbled Angela.

"I can't sleep in the dark," complained Laura. "Can't we have the light on?"

"There isn't a light. Go back to sleep!" sighed Angela.

They lay still for a while, listening to Maisie's loud snores.

"What if there are snakes?" said Laura. "What if a big snake gets into the tent while we're asleep?"

"There aren't any snakes," sighed
Angela.

THUMP!

Laura almost jumped out of her skin.

"What was that?" she yelped.

"Listen!"

THUMP. THUMP.

It sounded like something was moving around outside. The trouble with tents was there was no lock on the door.

"It's probably just the wind," Angela whispered.

"But what if it isn't?" moaned Laura. "What if it's a snake or wolf ... or a grizzly bear?"

SNAP!

There it was again, very close to the tent. Angela didn't think there were bears in the countryside, but you couldn't be certain. She shook Maisie awake.

"Mmm? Was going on?" mumbled Maisie, rolling over.

Angela put a finger to her lips. "SHHH! There's something outside!"

she whispered.

Maisie propped herself up on her elbows. The three of them held their breath.

"You imagined it," yawned Maisie, lying down again.

"We didn't!" whispered Laura. "We both heard it."

Angela found her torch and switched it on. Her face was ghostly white.

"Let's go and look," she said.

"What? *Out there?*" squeaked Laura.

"It's better than sitting here," said Angela. "With three of us, we can scare it off."

Angela unzipped the tent and they crawled out into the cold, dark night. The sky above them was full of stars.

Laura shivered. "Okay, we've looked. Let's go back inside now," she begged.

"Not until we've checked around," said Angela. She crept forward slowly. Her torchbeam picked out the ashes of their campfire. Over their heads the trees creaked in the wind. Laura held on to Angela's arm while Maisie picked up a stick just in case.

"TEE, HEE, HEE! SHH!"

Angela swung round. She was just in time to see two hooded figures scramble out of a tent and vanish into the dark.

"That's our tent!" said Angela. "Quick!"

They hurried back to their tent and crawled inside.

"My airbed's gone down!" moaned Maisie.

"Mine, too!" wailed Laura.

"And mine!" cried Angela.

She narrowed her eyes. Only one person could have done this.

Chapter 3

"ANGELA! WAKE UP!"

Angela blinked and opened her eyes. What was all the noise about?

She sat up in her sleeping bag. Bright sunlight dazzled her eyes. What was Brown Owl doing in their tent at this hour?

"It's gone nine, Angela!" said Brown

Owl. "All the other groups are up and dressed!"

Angela rubbed her eyes. Her back ached from sleeping on the rock hard ground. Laura and Maisie were huddled in their pyjamas looking sheepish. Brown Owl pointed at the clothes lying around.

"This tent is a mess!" she said. "Didn't I tell you to keep it tidy?"

"But … but we just woke up!" protested Angela.

"Then you should have set an alarm," said Brown Owl.

"It wasn't our fault!" grumbled Maisie. "Someone let down our airbeds and—"

"Don't tell stories," said Brown Owl. "Right, I'm taking marks off for today's

inspection. Tomorrow I'll expect a big improvement." She turned to go. "Oh, and you could learn a lot from Tiffany's group – their tent was spotless!" she said, striding off.

Angela poked her head out of the tent. Tiffany and Alice were outside, eavesdropping.

"Oh dear, ANG-ER-LA! Didn't you sleep well?" jeered Tiffany. "We got up early for tent inspection."

Angela scowled. "I know it was you last night and you won't get away with it," she said.

Tiffany did her wide-eyed "Miss Innocent" look.

"I don't know what you're talking about," she smirked. "Oh, and by the way, our tent got full marks, so there! I've always wanted a Camper badge, haven't you, Alice?"

Angela stuck out her tongue and ducked back into her tent.

Right, she thought, *if that's how you want to play, Tiffany, then you better watch out.*

During the day the girls learned camping skills such as collecting firewood and how to tell a toadstool from a mushroom (one made you sick, the other didn't).

That night Angela waited until the campsite was quiet, then found her torch and woke the others.

"Hurry up," she whispered. "We're going on a raid."

Maisie groaned. "Do we have to?"

Laura hid in her sleeping bag. "Can't I stay here? It's raining," she grumbled.

"Have you forgotten last night?" asked Angela. "We're not letting Tiffany's lot win. Come on!"

Laura and Maisie dragged themselves out of their sleeping bags and crawled outside into the drizzly rain. Angela led the way, shining her torch in the dark.

"What are we going to do?" whispered Laura.

"Same as they did," said Maisie. "Let down their airbeds."

Angela shook her head. "Oh no, I've got a better idea," she said.

Chapter 4

Angela shone her torch round the
circle of tents. The beam picked out
the largest tent, from which came
small snuffly snores.

"That's Tiffany all right," said Angela.
Even her snoring sounded polite.
When Maisie snored it sounded like
a hippopotamus.

Angela put a finger to her lips and quickly unzipped the tent. ZZZZZZZZIP!

Laura got ready to run, but the snoring went on. Tiffany was a sound sleeper. Angela switched off her torch and crawled into the tent with Maisie. Laura waited outside.

Inside, Angela could just make out three shapes in sleeping bags. On the nearest pillow she recognized Tiffany's blonde curls. Three piles of clothes were arranged in a neat line, ready for inspection.

Angela grabbed the pile nearest Tiffany's bed and dashed for the tent flap.

"Oww! Look where you're going!" hissed Maisie.

"SHH!" said Angela.

They scrambled out of the tent, almost knocking over Laura.

"So, what's the idea?" whispered Maisie, as they scurried away.

Angela held up the pile triumphantly. "They're Tiffany's clothes," she grinned. "Think about it. Tiffany will wake up tomorrow and find she's got nothing to wear. Imagine her face!"

They hurried back past the campfire. Angela stopped. Wait, they couldn't hide the clothes in their tent.

What if someone found them? No, it had to be somewhere else. Angela looked up. She'd just thought of the perfect place. This was going to be brilliant!

Next morning Angela was up bright and early, waiting for Tiffany to appear. Wouldn't she wail and scream when she saw where her clothes were?

Laura and Maisie crawled out of the tent.

"Is she up yet?" asked Maisie.

Just then, a tent was unzipped and Tiffany climbed out. Angela stared. Tiffany was fully dressed, wearing her sweatshirt, jogging bottoms and trainers.

"Something the matter, Angela?" she asked.

"N-no," replied Angela. "Um, is anything missing from your tent?"

"Oh, this isn't MY tent," said Tiffany.

"What?" said Angela.

"The rain dripped on my sleeping bag last night," said Tiffany. "So I moved in with Brown Owl and Tawny Owl."

Angela gulped. Then it wasn't Tiffany's tent they'd raided last night! And it couldn't have been Tiffany's clothes they'd taken, since she was wearing them. But in that case – whose clothes were they?

"ARGHHH!"

Brown Owl stormed out of her tent wearing her nightie and a pair of boots.

"HAS ANYONE SEEN MY CLOTHES?" she demanded. "They were…"

She broke off, catching sight of the clothes hanging from a tree – jumper, jeans, socks, vest, and frilly knickers – all dripping wet. Brown Owl pointed a finger.

"WHO DID THIS?" she bellowed.

"Oh, Ang-er-la, you've gone all red!" smirked Tiffany.

93

Brown Owl fixed Angela with a glare. "Angela Nicely, come here!" she yelled.

Angela and her friends had to peg out the soggy clothes and underwear to dry. Worse still, Brown Owl put them on washing-up duty for the rest of the day.

Angela sighed as she wiped another dirty breakfast bowl. How was she to know Tiffany had moved tents in the night? It wasn't fair!

Tiffany ran into the barn. "Hey, Brown Owl just finished inspection," she said. "Guess whose tent won?"

Angela groaned. "No idea," she said.

"MINE!" whooped Tiffany. "Well, Alice and Suki too, of course, but they just did what I told them."

"Congratulations," said Angela, banging down a bowl. The washing-up water needed changing.

"Thanks!" said Tiffany. "I'll show you my Camper badge if you like. Poor you, you've hardly got any badges and I've got *so* many!"

Angela gritted her teeth. That was it – she'd put up with all she could take.

"Have you got your Hair-washing badge?" she asked.

Tiffany frowned. "There isn't a Hair-washing badge."

"Pity," said Angela, emptying the washing-up water over her head.